AUSTRALIA

IN THE WORLD CRISIS
1929–1933

AUSTRALIA
IN THE WORLD CRISIS
1929—1933

THE ALFRED MARSHALL LECTURES
DELIVERED IN THE UNIVERSITY OF CAMBRIDGE
OCTOBER AND NOVEMBER 1933

By

DOUGLAS COPLAND

Professor of Commerce in the University of Melbourne

CAMBRIDGE

AT THE UNIVERSITY PRESS

1934

CAMBRIDGE UNIVERSITY PRESS
Cambridge, New York, Melbourne, Madrid, Cape Town,
Singapore, São Paulo, Delhi, Mexico City

Cambridge University Press
The Edinburgh Building, Cambridge CB2 8RU, UK

Published in the United States of America by Cambridge University Press, New York

www.cambridge.org
Information on this title: www.cambridge.org/9781107692862

© Cambridge University Press 1934

First published 1934
First paperback edition 2013

A catalogue record for this publication is available from the British Library

ISBN 978-1-107-69286-2 Paperback

TO
MY WIFE

PREFACE

AUSTRALIAN economic policy in the depression is in some respects an experiment. As such it will be of interest to economic students in general for the light it throws upon measures that may be taken to mitigate the disturbances of an economic depression and to promote recovery. At this stage the complete results cannot be assessed. Australia is now passing through a period of moderate recovery, and the progress of this movement is likely to be affected by a number of forces, some of a non-economic nature, that are at present indeterminate. In these circumstances it would be injudicious to claim too much for the experiment. All that can be said at this moment is that it has succeeded in reaching some of its more important immediate objectives.

I have drawn freely upon ideas that have emerged from frequent discussions with my Australian colleagues. I must, however, accept full responsibility for the argument advanced in the lectures. The book does not give a complete account of the Australian crisis. That is impossible in a course of eight lectures. All that can be claimed for it is that it attempts to present an outline of the problem and to sketch the main lines of policy pursued. A lecturer is in the happy position of choosing those elements of a problem that may have a wide appeal. He can escape the tedium of minute detail, though at a risk of ignoring facts that may upset his generalisations. I hope my free use of the lecturer's privilege of selection will not have led me into too many errors of omission, or committed me to hasty generalisations.

I am greatly indebted to Mr J. G. Norris, LL.M., for guidance in the legal aspects of the interest and rent reduction legislation and the moratorium legislation, to Miss Jean Polglaze, B.Com., for preparing the charts and statistical tables, and to Mr G. C. Billing for reading the manuscript and preparing the index.

D. B. COPLAND

LONDON

September 20, 1933

CONTENTS

xii   *Contents*

                                                    page
LIST OF CHARTS

DIARY OF THE AUSTRALIAN CRISIS

This diary of events in the Australian Crisis is not exhaustive. It is prepared for the convenience of students who attended the lectures and for readers not familiar with the order of events. A more comprehensive statement for the period July 1930 to November 1932 will be found in the *Commonwealth Year Book*, No. 25, pp. 841–5.

1929

August   Heavy fall in wool prices at Sydney sales. Long-term external borrowing had ceased and temporary relief was obtained in 1929 by issues of treasury bills of £10 m. on the London market and bank overdraft in London. Dissolution of Parliament after defeat of Government on proposal to abandon Commonwealth Arbitration Court.

October   Defeat of Bruce-Page Government at General Election and formation of Scullin (Labour) Government.

November   Legislation empowering Commonwealth Bank to mobilise gold reserves.

December   Beginning of heavy exports of gold reserves. Exchange rate on sterling at £1. 10s. 0d.% premium.

1930

March   Heavy increase of import duties, imposition of tariff embargoes and rationing of imports. Exchange premium at £6. 6s. 3d. %. (Raised on March 24th from £3. 16s. 3d. %.)

June   Economists' Statement on Economic Position—First Manifesto.

July— *August*	Visit of Sir Otto Niemeyer, representing Bank of England. Statement to Premiers' Conference on severely deflationary lines. Melbourne Agreement to balance budgets. Commonwealth sales tax of 6% imposed.
September	Formation of Exchange Pool. Outside market for exchange increasing and rate rising. Memorandum of Messrs Giblin, Dyason and Copland to Acting-Commonwealth Treasurer—A Plan for Economic Adjustment.
October	Victory of Labour at New South Wales elections, and formation of Lang Government. Exchange premium at £8. 15s. 0d.% and outside rate still rising above official rate.
November	Commonwealth budget policy inconsistent with Melbourne Agreement, despite efforts of Treasurer. Special super-tax of $7\frac{1}{2}$% on income from property.
1931 *January*	Economists' Statement—Second Manifesto. Declaration of 10% cut in real wages by Commonwealth Arbitration Court in Basic Wage Case.
January TO *February*	Premiers' Conference, Canberra and Melbourne. Treasury Officers' Report on Budget and Economic Position. The Lang Plan enunciated. Mr Theodore proposes policy of restoring 1929 price level. Decision of Loan Council to balance budgets in three years by economies and taxation of interest. Exchange premium on initiative of Bank of New South Wales rises rapidly and is finally fixed at £1 10s. 0d.%.

March TO *April*	Statement of inflationary policy by Mr Theodore. Letter of Chairman of Commonwealth Bank to Loan Council fixing limit of advances to Governments at £25 m. abroad, then reached, and £25 m. internal. Reply by Mr Theodore (Chairman of Loan Council) strongly criticising bank policy.
May	Appointment of Committee of Economists and Under-Treasurers (the Copland Committee) to advise Sub-Committee of Loan Council.
May 25 TO *June* 11	Report of Copland Committee. Premiers' Conference enunciates the Premiers' Plan. Amendment of Commonwealth Bank Act. Reduction in bank advances and deposit rates.
July—August	Reduction in treasury bill rate from 6% to 4%. Internal Conversion loan. Revision of Commonwealth Budget.
August—September	Premiers' Conference to review budget programme. Decision to convert compulsorily dissentients from Conversion loan holding 3% of total sum. Britain abandons gold standard.
October	Commonwealth Government decides to grant bounty of 4½d. per bushel to wheat growers.
November	Further reduction in bank deposit rates. Economists' Statement on Devaluation—Third Manifesto. Dissolution of Commonwealth Parliament.

4 *Diary of the Australian Crisis*

December Control of Exchange assumed by Commonwealth Bank.
Exchange premium fixed at £1. 5s. 0d. %.
State legislation for rent and interest adjustment completed.
Defeat of Commonwealth Government at elections.

1932
January Formation of Lyons Government.
Letter from Chairman of Commonwealth Bank to Prime Minister calling attention to growth of floating debt.
Premiers' Conference, Melbourne.

February Commencement of tariff revision; removal of prohibitions on imports.

March Further reductions in bank deposit rates.
The Financial Agreements (Commonwealth Liability) Act affirms liability of Commonwealth for State Debts.
The Financial Agreements Enforcement Act giving Commonwealth powers to attach State revenues.

April Report of Committee of Experts (Wallace Bruce Committee) appointed to make a "Preliminary Survey of the Economic Problem".
Premiers' Conference, Melbourne.

May Mr Lang dismissed by Governor of New South Wales.
Formation of Stevens Ministry.
Defeat of Victorian Labour Government at elections.

June Defeat of New South Wales Labour Party at elections.

June
(cont.)

Reconstitution of State Industrial Court in New South Wales.
Victory of Labour Party in Queensland elections.
Commonwealth Court refuses to restore special 10 % cut in basic wage.
Amendment of Commonwealth Bank Act.
Further reduction in bank deposit rates.

June—
July

Premiers' Conference reviews operation of Plan and agrees to aggregate State deficits of £9 m. for 1932/33.
Three-year special unemployment relief plan of £15 m. agreed to, and works programme of £6 m. for 1932/33.
Budget reform in New South Wales.

August

Reduction in New South Wales basic wage from £4. 2s. 6d. to £3. 10s. 0d.

September

Reductions in taxation and in pensions by Commonwealth.
Removal of remaining prohibitions on imports.

October

New Commonwealth Consolidated 4 % stock at par.
Premiers' Conference: Controversy over funding proposal.
Decision to raise internal loan of £8 m. at 3¾ %.
Reduction in treasury bill rate from 4 % to 3½ %.

November

Further reduction in bank deposit rates.
Commonwealth reduces land and income tax, and announces bounties to primary producers, especially wheat growers, of £2·25 m.
New South Wales Conversion loan, £12·36 m., in London, from 5¾ % to 3½ % at 97½, maturing 1936/37.

1933

January   Further reduction in treasury bill rate.

Premiers' Conference, Melbourne, decides to finance loan works from public loans and to fund treasury bills if further loans possible at low rates of interest.

February Further reductions in bank deposit rate, and in treasury bill rate.

Conversion of New South Wales 4% loan of £9·62 m. in London to 4% at par, maturing 1955–70.

May   Commonwealth Arbitration Court refuses to restore special 10% cut in basic wage but accepts "all items" index number as basis for wage adjustment to cost of living in lieu of food, groceries and house rents index number.

Defeat of Labour Government in South Australian elections.

Victory of Labour Party in Western Australian elections.

Conversion of 6½% State loans of £11·41 m. in London to 3½% at 99, maturing 1937/38.

May–   Premiers' Conference decides to issue internal
June   loan at 3¾% and to fix State deficits for 1933/34 at £8·5 m.

Reductions in tariff.

Further reduction in treasury bill rate to 2½%.

Internal loan over-subscribed.

July   Conversion of State 6% loans, aggregating £17·22 m. in London, to 4% at 99, maturing 1943–48.

Surplus of £3·5 m. in Commonwealth Budget for 1932/33.

July
(cont.)
Deficit of £8·5 m. in State budgets for 1932/33 compared with £9 m. agreed upon and £21 m. for 1931/32.

August Rise in wool prices.

September Conversion of £15 m. 6% Commonwealth loans and £5·95 m. 5¾% State loans in London to 3¾% at 98, maturing 1948–53.

Heavy reductions in Commonwealth taxation announced in Budget.

Reduction of primage and import duties on British goods to a maximum of 17½%.

I

BASIS OF AUSTRALIAN PROSPERITY—
1925 TO 1929

I. *Special interest of the Australian Problem*

MY predecessor in this Lectureship (Sir Arthur Salter) spoke to you last year about the basic conditions of a planned society. It has fallen to my lot in the past three years to assist in the formulation and carrying out of a plan of swift adjustment of the economic life of a country that was among the first to feel the impact of the great depression that gripped the world from 1930 to, shall we say, 1933. There is much in this experience of Australia of interest both to those who desire to make plans for a new economic order, and to those who wish to bend the existing economic order to the conditions imposed by the depression. It is with the more restricted interests of the latter group that I am most concerned in these Lectures. The grand theme of planning may be left to others, but I may be permitted to make one comment. We had much planning in Australia before 1929, and our critics of 1930 were wise after the event.

Much has happened since 1930. The world has learnt that no economic order was immune from the destructive forces that struck Australia in 1930. The disasters that engulfed one nation after another in quick succession have done more to expose the weaknesses of economic organisation than half a century's logical criticism. If we move out of this depression with nothing but the memory of disorder and suffering, we can scarcely expect the common man to retain his respect for an economic society that cannot offer him continuity of an ordered life.

Is there nothing in the experience of the depression that throws light on this old problem? Can we avoid the recurrence of economic and social disorders associated with depressions? If we cannot eliminate the depression, can we mitigate its severity and hasten the recovery? It is because I think that Australian experience in the past three years can throw some light on these questions that I have accepted the invitation to deliver these Alfred Marshall Lectures.

The subject is one that would have engaged the interest of Marshall. It has those elements of quantitative analysis, of experiment, and of deep social significance that would have offered great scope for his constructive genius. One can imagine the extraordinary enthusiasm Marshall would have shown for a people capable of carrying through a bold and unorthodox policy at a time when most other countries either refused to take stern measures, or sought to conceal from their people the facts of the depression. It has been said in reproach that Australia was forced to act. This is not strictly true, and it covers up an important fact. Australia refused to take the half-measures of deflation that are usually recommended to countries in similar difficulties. That was deliberate choice. She also refused to pursue the course of inflation taken by so many nations after the war. That also was deliberate choice. She pursued a middle course that had not hitherto been fully explored. It was the inherent fairness of this course that appealed to people. Marshall would have felt the force of this appeal all the more because it combined a large element of social justice with sound economic effort. The full significance for economic theory of this special feature of Australian policy must be left to those whose vision penetrates deeper than mine. I confine myself largely to an *exposé* of the experiment and will add such comments on broader and more fundamental issues in theory as occur to me. One who has lived through the excitement of Australian economic policy in recent years may know the story without appreciating its full significance.

II. *Importance of External Influences*

We commence with the conditions of prosperity from 1925 to 1929. This is a period typical of Australian pre-depression policy. The country was undoubtedly prosperous in these years, though there was some national soul searching concerning the basis and duration of that prosperity. High export prices, a growing volume of exports and a fairly regular but excessive inflow of capital were the basic conditions of prosperity. On the eve of the crisis, Australia had an income from abroad of about £140 m. from exports and £30 m. from Government long-term borrowing. The total of £170 m. was a little more than 25 % of estimated national income. In short periods this ratio could not change. Nothing in Australian policy in the period 1925–29 caused a fundamental change in the ratio. Year to year variations in income from *exports* were offset by credit policy familiar in a country where banks finance export industries subject to large annual movements in both price and volume. Similarly, year to year variations in income from *long-term borrowing* were offset by credit policy in London, where overdrafts were obtained on loan account pending the issue of a long-term loan.[1]

It is not my purpose here to examine internal movements that would modify temporarily the effects of "income from overseas" on the Australian economy. If this income were available as a regular inflow at a high level it would have an important stabilising influence upon internal conditions. This was the situation from 1925 to 1929. It was an era of high prices for raw materials and food-stuffs, of

[1] Witness the expression "arrears of borrowing" used in treasury circles in Australia to explain heavily overdrawn accounts.

buoyant conditions in the overseas loan markets, and of great capital expenditure. Australia ate of the fruits of this prosperity as much as most countries, not because Australian policy was especially designed to obtain a good share of the fruits, but because she was a new country with attractions for the investor, and with exports that always bring high prices in a period of heavy world capital expenditure. In these circumstances external forces were far more important than internal. How would Australia's national income be affected by an expansion of export production or by an addition to export income following a rise in export prices? This, I well remember, was our fundamental problem in those days. The answer was given by a simple series showing that the export producer spent two-thirds of his outgo on domestic goods, and one-third on imported goods. This was true of all producers. Hence the two-thirds was again split up in the same ratio, and so on. So we got a series:

$$1 + 2/3 + (2/3)^2 + (2/3)^3 + \ldots = 3.$$

Thus for every £100 added to export production the addition to national income was £300.[1] Higher prices as well as expansion of volume increased national income and sustained prosperity. Capital imports also made for higher national income during the period of their expenditure. Credit expansion in Australia would act in the same direction, but it was not as potent a factor as the external forces. Banking policy before the depression was intimately related to the balance of payments and was the passive rather than the active element of the relationship. Internal loans for public works were only half as great as external and were financed from current saving. Deliberate policy on the part

[1] This problem was first carefully considered in enquiries made in 1928 by the Development and Migration Commission when investigating a railway project in Victoria. It was expounded more fully in Giblin, *Australia*, 1930, *An Inaugural Lecture*. It is not the same problem as how much is added to national income by an addition to "export income" as defined above.

of Australia in promoting prosperity before the depression was therefore largely confined to overseas borrowing and the expansion of export production. To a considerable extent they are related as cause and effect. Since increased export production seemed an enduring monument to enterprise, overseas borrowing was good to the extent to which it increased Australia's capacity to export. The rest was a burden of dead weight debt. Its temporary stimulus to enterprise only masked for a time its deleterious effects. When the stimulus was spent the burden became greater by contrast.

When the depression hit Australia, the bad effects of this borrowing policy were exaggerated by critics both at home and abroad. It was associated with criticism of high protection and wage fixation. Australia had worshipped false economic gods for many years. 1930 was her Nemesis. These were the beliefs of many people in Australia and I do not recall them in any petulant outburst against overseas critics. These critics were indeed not without support among Australian authorities, as may be shown by considering the trend of economic thought in Australia in the five years before the crisis. This trend may most conveniently be indicated in a discussion of the strength and weakness of the economic situation in the period 1925–29. We proceed to this discussion in the remaining sections of this Lecture.

III. *Terms of Trade and Overseas Borrowing*

If we look more closely into economic conditions in the favourable years 1925 to 1929 we find that up to the middle of 1929 Australia was favoured by a combination of circumstances that enabled the traditional policy of rapid development to be pursued with all the outward signs of success. First, wool prices were high and the clip increased steadily in volume. Wheat prices were equally satisfactory and there was a considerable expansion of production.[1] The less important exports were on the whole favoured by satisfactory overseas prices and total exports were sustained at approximately £145 m. per annum from 1926/27 to 1928/29 compared with £120 m. for the years 1921/22 to 1923/24. Statistics for wool and wheat may be given in detail.

ANNUAL AVERAGE

	1921/22 to 1923/24	1926/27 to 1928/29	Percentage increase
WOOL	m.	m.	
No. of sheep	84·3	103·4	23
Wool produced (lb.)	703	927	30
Value of clip	£53·7	£71·9	32
WHEAT			
Acreage	9·6	12·9	34
Total yield (bushels)	121	146	20
Value of crop	£31·2	£37·5	20

The principal primary industries had thus experienced an increase in output equivalent to the increase in value.

	Export prices (1911, 100)	Import prices (1911, 100)	Terms of trade (1911, 100)
1920	194	280	69
1921	171	214	79
1922	162	195	83
1923	194	199	97
1924	228	197	116
1925	214	184	116
1926	183	174	105
1927	186	174	107
1928	185	175	106
1929	158	173	90*

* This is perhaps too low. Export prices were published for trade years and I obtained calendar years by averaging two successive years. It was not till the middle of 1929 that export prices slumped heavily and my method of estimating tends to under-state the export price level for 1929.

[1] Sections III and IV are reproduced with slight modifications from my article on "The Australian Problem" in *The Economic Journal* for December 1930.

Secondly, the terms of international trade were in favour of Australia. The Commonwealth Statistician constructs an index number of export prices and the Government Statistician of New South Wales an index number of import prices for that State.[1] The movements in these index numbers for some years were as given above (p. 14).

The ratio of international exchange was thus moving in favour of Australia up to 1925, and it was still favourable in 1928.

Thirdly, Australia was able to raise substantial loans overseas. At June 30th, 1923, the external debt was £419·6 m. and it had risen to £570 m. by June 30th, 1928, an increase of £30 m. per annum. This influx of capital was a powerful influence in sustaining prosperity, but in view of the facts recorded above concerning the export trades and the ratio of international exchange, it would be an error to attribute the high level of prosperity up to 1928 wholly to overseas borrowing. The rate of borrowing was, however, excessive, and there were indications both in Australia and in London that some reduction must take place. The interest burden on the external debt in this period rose from £19·1 m. to £27·6 m., an increase of 44% compared with an increase of 36% in the debt, a clear indication that borrowing was becoming more costly. The ratio of interest payments to the value of exports and recorded production (estimated to be about two-thirds of national income) was as follows:

PERCENTAGE EXTERNAL INTEREST TO

	(a) Exports	(b) Production
1913	9·5	3·4
1923	16·2	5·0
1928	19·5	6·0
1929	19·2	6·1

[1] The utility of this index number as a measure of import prices is discussed in Benham, *The Prosperity of Australia*, pp. 251–5.

The situation disclosed by these percentages was becoming precarious even with the satisfactory condition of export production. While overseas borrowing continued the transfer problem was not difficult, a condition familiar to all debtor countries since the war. To meet interest payments on the overseas debt Australia had in 1929 a transfer problem amounting to nearly £4. 10s. per head, much higher than Germany and any other country except New Zealand. It was the magnitude of this transfer problem that caused concern to competent observers of the economic conditions of Australia even in the days of prosperity.

IV. *Structural Weaknesses*

But it was not the only danger spot in the position. Four others must be mentioned. First, the development of industry was depending more and more upon the tariff and other forms of assistance. Taking the average of the years 1911/12 to 1913/14 and 1924/25 to 1926/27 employment of males in all rural industries increased by 4% compared with 38% for manufacturing industry. Manufacturing production increased from 26% of total production in 1913 to 35% in 1927/28 and 36% in 1928/29. This was a natural development in a country that had first pursued primary production and later turned to secondary industries. But the development was somewhat forced. Only two primary industries had shown a substantial increase in males employed in the period above-mentioned. These were dairying and sugar, both favoured by the tariff. In manufacturing the greatest increases had occurred in protected industry, and the increase was roughly proportional to the degree of assistance given. Obviously, development of this kind is costly and throws a heavy burden upon export industries. The Tariff Committee, appointed by the Prime Minister, reported in 1929 that the cost to the export industries was from 8% to 10% in 1926/27, and it viewed any increase with concern.[1]

Secondly, the Australian price level had remained at approximately the level it reached after the post-war deflation. U.S.A. prices were lower relatively to the 1913 position and British prices fell continuously from 1924. In 1928, British prices as measured by the Board of Trade index number were about 33% above pre-war levels, while Australian were 65% up. Whilst these figures cannot be taken as an accurate measure of the disparity in price movements in Australia and overseas, there is no doubt that the Australian price level was sustained at a high figure, while overseas prices were either falling or stable at a lower level. Two main causes account for this disparity. First, the overseas borrowing increased spending power and the volume of bank credits, and, secondly, the high prices for Australian exports were reflected in high internal prices. The tariff was, of course, a contributing factor in keeping up the prices of manufactured and sheltered goods, but in the absence of the other two main causes the tariff could not have sustained high prices without forcing a contraction of export production and a decline in real wages.

Thirdly, the general level of wages was rising. In 1922, there was added to the basic wage what came to be known as the Powers' 3s. This was intended to compensate for the losses incurred by wage earners on account of the rise in the

[1] See *The Australian Tariff: An Economic Enquiry*, Part VI. On p. 87 the Committee stated "Our surplus resources available to subsidize industry are limited and will not stand any greater strain than imposed by the present tariff". In spite of efforts to develop secondary industries and to stimulate immigration by loan expenditure the rate of growth of population was falling after 1920. The natural increase declined from 1·5% in 1920 to 1·2% in 1928. Immigration was high from 1922 to 1927 and for the eight years ending June 30th, 1929, accounted for 0·55% per annum increase in population. This is equivalent to the rate of increase from this source before the war, but immigration declined after 1928 and in 1931 there was a net emigration. Present trend of population indicates that the rate of economic progress in Australia will be less in the immediate future than it was either before or after the war.

cost of living and the lag in the adjustment of wages, but it was continued after the reason for it had disappeared. Owing to the increase in the number of workers brought within the ambit of arbitration and wage-fixing tribunals, including many engaged in state instrumentalities, the basic wage was applied to a larger number of workers. The adjustments in the basic wage were made on the basis of an index number of retail prices of food and house rents, estimated to cover about 60% of household expenditure. This index number had not fallen in 1930 to the same extent as a more complete index number, including clothing and other household expenditure. Had the basic wage been adjusted according to movements in the more complete index number, "the Harvester equivalent" (the standard fixed by Mr Justice Higgins in 1907) could have been observed in 1930 with a basic wage 6% less than that in operation. The steady upward trend of unemployment up to 1929 must be regarded as an indication of the development of wage rates somewhat beyond the capacity of industry. The average unemployment for the years 1922–29 was 10% with a rising tendency. If unemployment is ignored real wages were 8% higher in 1929 than in 1911, but when allowance is made for the incidence of unemployment the real wage was barely 1% higher.[1]

Fourthly, the condition of public finance was becoming unsatisfactory. Commonwealth revenue had been buoyant during the period of high imports, and the Commonwealth Government increased expenditure on schemes of development such as Federal aid to roads involving £2 m. per annum. With the decline in imports and customs revenue and the increasing burden of interest payments, deficits in the Commonwealth accounts commenced to make their appearance, and at June 30th, 1930, a deficit of £6·5 m.

[1] *Labour Report*, No. 20, 1929 (Commonwealth Bureau of Census and Statistics), p. 81.

had been accumulated. The position in the States was much more difficult on account of the heavy loan expenditure on public undertakings. Sir Lennon Raws, in *The Economic Record* for November 1928, made a comprehensive statement of Australian loan expenditure. He found that at June 1927 the total capital expenditure on public undertakings including railways had amounted to a little over £400 m. The financial returns for the year showed a deficit of $1\frac{1}{2}$% on this capital. It was the increasing burden of interest payments that compromised the State budgets. This may be indicated from the following table (figures in millions):

Year	Interest on State debts	Interest on Commonwealth debt	State taxation	Commonwealth taxation	Value of recorded production
	£ m.	£ m.	£ m.	£ m.	£ m.
1923	25·5	17·3	19·0	49·9	379·4
1925	29·2	17·6	22·9	52·8	454·1
1928	35·6	19·5	31·2	56·6	453·3
1929	35·9	19·6	32·4	56·3	447·8

It is clear from this table that the percentage of interest payments and taxation to production had been steadily rising during the period. The increase in interest was due in part to an increase in the total public debt from £905 m. in 1923 to £1104 m. in 1929, and in part to the increase in the rate of interest payable on the debt. The average rate on the State debts rose from £4. 13*s*. 2*d*. % in 1923 to £4. 18*s*. 11*d*. % in 1929, and for the Commonwealth debt from £4. 19*s*. 3*d*. % in 1923 to £5. 5*s*. % in 1929.

V. *Revisionist Policy*

Under the stimulus of high export prices, expansion of the volume of exports and heavy external borrowing, the money value of national income continued to expand, though at a declining rate, up to the eve of the depression. The estimates of national income most commonly used are those of

MrJ. T. Sutcliffe.[1] His method has been subject to criticism and review but other methods have not produced widely different results in the aggregate. For 1922/23 his estimate is £540 m. With minor fluctuations the estimate on the same basis rose steadily and reached a maximum of £650 m. for 1927/28 and fell a little to £645 m. for 1928/29. Since the estimate is based upon a fairly constant relation to value of production, it may be of interest to set out the movements in exports, "recorded" production and national income for the post-war period:

Year ending June 30th	Exports	Pro- duction	Income	Ratio of exports to	
				(a) Production	(b) Income
	£ m.	£ m.	£ m.	%	%
1923	118	379	540	31·1	21·9
1924	119	400	601	29·8	19·8
1925	163	455	641	35·8	25·5
1926	143	431	615	33·2	22·6
1927	136	447	641	30·4	21·2
1928	142	453	650	31·3	21·8
1929	144	448	645	32·1	21·5

There are considerable yearly fluctuations in the ratios, but over the whole period they tend to be stable. This is to be expected in a period when overseas borrowing was fairly stable and little change took place in the relative importance of secondary industry and export production. Provided the price level of exports held, there need be little fear of a sudden collapse of income, for in these circumstances overseas borrowing would not have ceased suddenly. A gradual decline could have been accomplished without causing serious disorganisation in domestic industry. That the authorities thought such a decline was necessary is shown by the establishment in 1928 of the Loan Council, with its contemplated control of and restriction of borrowing, and

[1] *The National Dividend* (Melbourne University Press), 1925.

the invitation to a British Mission to survey the economic position of Australia.[1] The Mission could not escape the conclusion that Australia had mortgaged her future too heavily, but it did not take a grave view of the situation. The Development and Migration Commission, established in 1926 to supervise the expenditure of loans under the "£34,000,000 Agreement" with the British Government, found on close investigation that many forms of capital expenditure were uneconomic. After five years of work it had been able to recommend the expenditure of only £6 m., and its later reports showed that it thought loan expenditure should be curbed.[2] Had the costs and benefits of all loan expenditure from 1926 been submitted to the same scrutiny as that proposed under the Agreement, the growth of the public debt would have been retarded.

Doubts also began to spread concerning the costs and benefits of another element of Australian economic policy, namely, protection. The Prime Minister in 1928 asked a Committee of five economists to report upon the tariff and its effects. Reference has already been made to the work of this Committee. It is only necessary to add here that the report was important for two reasons. It drew attention to the limits of successful application of the tariff and laid down principles upon which the tariff should be administered. Later this report influenced the work of the Tariff Board, but already in 1929 the Board was becoming restive about the high costs in protected industries.[3]

---

[1] See Report of the British Economic Mission to Australia, 1929.

[2] It was anticipated that the £34 m. would be spent in ten years and that 450,000 immigrants would be settled in this period. This fixes a capital requirement per immigrant of £75. This was quite contrary to experience, which indicated £300 as a low estimate. But it was traditional for both the British and Australian Governments to under-estimate the costs of immigration.

[3] See Annual Report of the Tariff Board for 1929. For the failure of employment to respond readily to capital expenditure and protection, see my article "The Tariff and Employment in Australia" in *Weltwirtschaftliches Archiv*, January 1933, and *The Peopling of Australia*, Further Studies (Melbourne University Press), 1933.

VI. *Australian Response to World Prosperity*

By participating so fully in the world boom of 1925 to 1929, Australia was, of course, exposing her economy to the same structural defects as were the investing countries in which the boom conditions originated. There was too much capital expansion, both public and private. Investment for the moment outran savings with familiar results. Capital equipment—roads, harbours, irrigation works, factories, theatres, etc.—went beyond the consumption requirements. There is ample evidence of this in the reports of the Tariff Board, which frequently refers to the equipment of industry being far in excess of what was necessary to supply the local market. Dr Mauldon has shown how greatly over-capacity in coal-mining embarrassed that industry, though this was perhaps hardly a product of the boom years.[1] In the cinema industry the reorganisation that took place during the depression revealed a condition of extravagant capital expenditure in the boom period. This growth of investment appeared top-heavy when the depression came on with full force. Investment would not have gone so far had there been no driving force from outside. It would not have appeared so extravagant had there been no world catastrophe. Australia was in fact a dependent economy, but a willing recipient, and even petitioner for a share in the boom conditions. But neither Australia nor the outside world expected export prices to fall so severely or long-term borrowing to be suddenly cut off. With a moderate recession of prices and reduction of borrowing, structural defects in the Australian economy would have become obvious to every eye. But they would not have appeared in the form of what was well-nigh an economic and social disaster. A business recession and some reduction in the standard of living were inevitable. The transfer of some labour from

[1] *The Economics of Australian Coal* (Melbourne University Press).

constructional industry to production of goods for current
consumption at home or abroad would have been accomplished by the fall in costs made possible by the suggested
fall in the standard of living. Whether this might have been
accomplished by direct cutting of costs or depreciation of
the currency is a point we need not decide here. It is
sufficient to have indicated the degree of adjustment required, despite structural defects, had there been no
dramatic collapse of export prices and no sudden termina-
tion of overseas borrowing.

There is thus much evidence to support critics who declared that the policy of Australia was fundamentally unsound, and that the disorder of 1930 and 1931 was the
inevitable result. I have already shown that the critics
were wrong in this view, but there is one further comment
to be made. We must distinguish between the failure of a
long-period policy and the breaking up of short-period
prosperity. The latter is the normal operation of the business
cycle, the former a special long-period influence that might
increase the oscillations of the cycle. But the great prosperity of 1925 to 1929 was not caused wholly by borrowing
and tariff policy. Similarly, the acute depression of 1930
and 1931 was not traceable to the failure of borrowing to
stimulate sufficient expansion of production, or to the
tendency of protection to establish high costs in secondary
industry with harmful effects on export industry. Had no
depression occurred some modification of traditional policy
was inevitable, and Australia was being prepared for this
change by criticism and constructive argument, both at
home and abroad.

We cannot ignore the effects of traditional economic
policy. It increased the normal troubles of depression and
made the problem of adjustment all the greater. But
Australia was not suffering in 1930 and 1931 so much
from the weakness of her own policy as from the general

depression that was rapidly spreading over the economic world. We have therefore to consider primarily a business depression in Australia. It was unusually severe, not because it came when Australia was about to meet the costs of mistakes in her economic policy, but because the external forces that caused the depression were much stronger than usual.

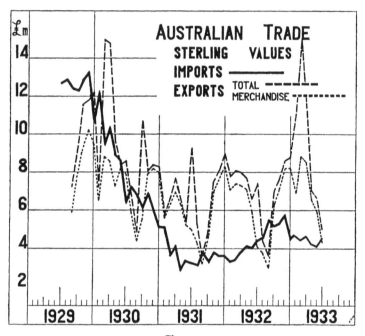

Chart 1

It is not part of my task to deal with the causes of the world economic depression. Australia was still a "dependent economy" in 1929, and she was in that group of countries producing raw materials and vegetable foodstuffs, the prices of which collapsed first in the depression. She was also vitally affected by the sudden cessation of overseas lending. The causes of these changes originated, in the main, outside Australia, and do not directly concern us, except in explaining the severity of the changes themselves. The boom of 1925 to 1929 was a great investment boom, one of the greatest in history. Because Australia was a producer of primary products and a market for capital, her economy quickly responded to boom conditions. For the same reasons her economy reacted to the depression with dramatic suddenness. Being a great governmental debtor and experiencing difficulties in "transfer", her position attracted much attention throughout the world. But it was not more serious than other countries with similar conditions, e.g. Brazil and Malaya. Soon it was to be not less serious than other primary producing countries with a greater proportion of exports of animal food-stuffs, the prices of which fell later. The case of New Zealand and of the Argentine are of special interest in this connection. But by the time these countries were drawn into the maelstrom, the whole world was in the grip of depression. Budget deficits, unemployment, transfer difficulties, credit stringency, currency depreciation, were then horses of a different colour. Australia had an advantage in coming into the depression early when it was customary, even in Australia and to a much greater extent abroad, to regard economic troubles as a measure of the errors of national policy. She was forced, as a distinguished visitor to her shores remarked, "to help herself".

VII. *Some Preparations for Adversity*

The story of her effort is one of the few cheerful episodes of the depression period. Had the prosperity of 1925 to 1929 been wholly unsound, Australia could not have made this successful effort. That she had joined with other countries in wasteful capital expenditure and in special policy to maintain an uneconomic standard of living is freely admitted. But the critic must take note of certain developments in this period of prosperity that were to operate much to Australia's advantage later. In the first place, the machinery of national economic administration was greatly improved. We have to deal with this in detail in Lecture IV. Here I desire merely to draw attention to (*a*) the Financial Agreement of 1928 and the Amendment of the Constitution that made it possible, (*b*) the Loan Council and its wide powers, (*c*) the new charter of the Commonwealth Bank, and (*d*) the amendments made in the Arbitration Act. All these were to have a pronounced influence upon the economic policy of Australia in the depression. In the second place, Australia did not waste all her gains from the era of prosperity. She had very substantial exchange reserves (London funds and internal gold reserves). Banking policy was responsible for this, not only the policy of the Commonwealth Bank, but also the policy of the trading banks. These reserves were quickly absorbed in the early stages of the depression, but they held the external position during the period occupied in preparing an aggressive and generally acceptable depression policy. In the third place, there was an expansion of export production and of protected production competing with imports. True, this expansion fell far short of what was desired, or what was necessary for meeting the permanent costs of development. But the community had a capital equipment that was available for handling a greater output without any addition to overhead costs. But greater output in export production was soon to be achieved, and it was in part made possible by the developmental policy of the era of prosperity. In the fourth place, the savings of the people through savings banks, insurance companies, friendly societies and housing were much greater than was realised before the depression. These savings were invested, on the whole, with prudence, though towards the end of the boom some doubtful mortgage finance was creeping into the policy of even staid financial institutions. The major weakness in the investment of savings was the association of rural credit operations with some savings banks. In general the high level of savings among the people, and their prudent investment by institutions, made for political and financial stability, even in the worst phases of the crisis. At any time from March 1930 to March 1931 strict accountancy would have reduced most financial institutions to a condition of insolvency, but strict accountancy in a crisis is a dangerous weapon in the hands of economic amateurs. On the canons of strict accountancy, all nations were hopelessly bankrupt at the end of 1931. A strict balance sheet of assets and liabilities would have promoted almost universal panic. This was avoided in Australia, not because the assets of most financial institutions had not shrunk to a small fraction of liabilities, but because both the debtor and the creditor had his attention directed to a policy that would preserve the money value of assets.

These internal developments greatly strengthened the ability of Australia to withstand the first shock of the crisis. They also provided machinery that could be used to give an element of flexibility to economic institutions. Thus the economic structure could be moulded in response to the heavy pressure imposed upon it by the crisis. In respect of machinery for control, especially, Australia builded better than she knew. The use she made of her new or reformed economic institutions after 1929 astonished her own people perhaps even more than her friends overseas.

II

THE IMPACT OF THE CRISIS—
LOSS OF INCOME

I. *The Concept of National Income*

AUSTRALIAN economic policy in the depression has two distinct phases—the first of expediency, the second of ordered plan. The adoption of the Premiers' Plan in June 1931 marks the end of the first phase of hastily devised expedients. Not unlike the Allies in the war, Australia was ill prepared to meet a resolute foe. There was much controversy and delay before a successful offensive could be launched, and it was planned only after traditional methods of attack had been to a large extent discarded and new weapons devised. Australians earned a reputation during the war for bold and unorthodox strategy. Their economic struggle of 1930 and 1931 gave them opportunity to show once more those qualities that made their shock tactics so successful in the war. But nearly two years of preparation were required before a dramatic advance along the whole economic front was possible. We are concerned in this lecture with this period of preparation.

It was in the many discussions of the impact of the crisis that plans for the advance were worked out. To the economists the problem of the crisis for Australia was one of loss of national income, the impact of that loss, the spreading of the loss, and the restoration of balance among the several groups of producers. Economic discussions had emphasised the concept of national income before the depression. This was necessary because many elements of Australian policy—wage fixation, tariff, immigration, borrowing, social expenditure—had to be tested by their effects on national income. I need not develop this point here. Ample evidence of the emphasis of Australian economists upon national income can be found in the Tariff Report of a Committee of five economists, *The Australian Tariff: An Economic Enquiry*, and in the pages of the newly established Journal of the Economic Society of Australia and New Zealand, *The Economic Record*. Economists were agreed upon the amount and nature of national income. When the depression occurred they at once began to consider the effects upon not only the amount, but also the distribution of national income. They discussed the problem among themselves, with political leaders, and with the public.

This venture in the economic education of a people in a depression had unexpected results. The concept of national income became familiar to all thinking people. I remember one of my colleagues returning early in 1931 after a year's absence abroad, and being greatly impressed by what appeared at the moment as a somewhat trivial incident. On the day of his return, he and I were waiting on a railway station when a stranger approached me and begged leave to ask a question about the national income. He was a railway clerk and the subject had been freely discussed in his office. Was his salary part of the national income? There ensued five minutes of quite intelligent conversation on the subject, and the young man went away, as far as we could judge, accepting some loss of salary as inevitable and fair in the circumstances. It was the general acceptance of this point of view that was the real achievement during the first phase of Australian economic policy.

II. *First Reactions: Tariff and Exchange Policy*

I return to an estimate of the loss of income later in this lecture. We consider now the first impact of the crisis on Australian opinion and policy. Bear in mind that in August 1929 the country had rejected summarily a proposal to abolish one of the cherished institutions of industrial democracy—the Commonwealth Court of Conciliation and Arbitration. The proposal was regarded as a blow at the standard of living, and a Commonwealth Government was returned with an overwhelming majority pledged to safeguard that standard of living at all costs. The crisis was

AUSTRALIAN EXPORT PRICE INDEX
1928 = 100
AUSTRALIAN CURRENCY ————
STERLING — — — — — — —
GOLD ‥‥‥‥‥‥‥

Chart 2

then only a small cloud on the horizon. Long-term borrowing had ceased, and accommodation was obtained in London only by two issues of treasury bills of £5 m. each, at very high rates. It was the opening of the export season, and wool, metal and wheat prices had commenced their downward career. Loss of income was only in prospect. It had not yet occurred, either from cessation of borrowing or from low export prices. When it did occur it fell at first on a few groups—export producers, recipients of profits, owners of equity securities, and the unemployed. The internal disorganisation and distress to come was perceived by few, and under-estimated by all. But there was already a difficult external situation, and it rapidly assumed a major crisis.

It was too early in the crisis to secure any general endorsement of the view that the loss of income would inevitably spread to all classes. If Australia were to suffer from reduction of overseas loans and lower export prices, that problem could be met by reducing imports and using gold and foreign exchange reserves during the period required to adjust the balance of payments. That at least appeared to be the official view of the Government. The first step, therefore, was to pass legislation empowering the Commonwealth Bank to acquire, on behalf of the Government, gold reserves held by the private banks. These amounted in June 1929 to about £25 m. The Commonwealth Bank held another £22 m., and there was an estimated amount of £43 m. of exchange reserves in London. The total was £90 m. It was a splendid reserve fund and was freely drawn upon, for in 1929/30 gold exports amounted to £28 m. and the short-term indebtedness of the Governments to the Commonwealth Bank in London had increased to £18 m. It was, however, a mistaken policy to use external reserves so freely, while nothing was done to correct a domestic situation that required so liberal a use of reserves. Though Australia was technically off the gold standard at the end of 1929 every effort was made to preserve parity of the Australian pound with sterling. You are all familiar with the elementary principle that an over-valuation of a currency in the early stages of a crisis is a grave handicap to economic adjustment.[1]

---

[1] The problems of the balance of payments and currency depreciation are discussed in Lecture V.

The second step in correcting the external position was to increase early in 1930 the already heavy import duties, and to impose prohibitions on some luxury imports. This step was officially justified on the double ground of checking imports and providing employment. That it was a false step is capable of ready demonstration. The tariff enquiry of 1929 had shown that tariff costs were retarding the growth of export production. They amounted to 9 % of costs on the whole in export industries. Higher tariffs at the moment merely served to sustain high prices in protected industry, and thus to support a level of costs for export industry that added to the rapidly growing difficulties of export producers. It was, moreover, a clumsy and tardy method of reducing imports. In 1929/30 imports were still £131 m. compared with £144 m. in 1928/29, but exports had fallen from £140 m. to £97 m. The theory behind the tariff policy of the moment was indeed wholly fallacious. Imports would have fallen more rapidly had the currency not been over-valued, and the volume of credit for importers been restricted earlier. The higher tariff like the exploitation of exchange and gold reserves did nothing to check the forces of economic deterioration. On the contrary, it imposed fresh difficulties and diverted attention from the real task of economic adjustment.

III. *Increasing Internal Difficulties*

It was, of course, a fundamental mistake to assume that the external problem could be divorced from the internal. The mere shutting out of imports and the use of reserves to meet overseas obligations could not solve any fundamental problem. Special measures had to be devised to meet the "transfer" difficulty during the process of internal economic adjustment. It was a mistake to concentrate on these measures while internal policy was aggravating the difficulties of transfer. Public expenditure was being maintained, industrial wages were still unchanged for workers in employment, interest and rent at the old levels were still being paid, prices for sheltered and protected goods and services were still high, and the currency was over-valued. All this tended to maintain imports and to crush the export trades. So much did the external problem engage the attention of the authorities that as late as September 1930, when little had been done internally, an exchange pool was established in the belief that this would guarantee the service of the external debt. Fortunately, it was not a compulsory pool with a licensing system for exports. The country was saved this piece of folly that tied so many countries to a policy of deflation and over-valuation of currency. The pool still exists nominally, but it is not necessary. The service of the external debt cannot be met permanently in any country by regulations that cramp internal enterprise, and deny exporters their much-needed relief from a free exchange market that depreciates a currency.

But however much the external problem might engage official attention, the pressure of economic facts soon exposed the weakness of expedients that offered temporary relief externally, and served but to aggravate internal difficulties. Ominous signs of a disordered economy were not wanting. *In finance* the bond market was sagging and the average rate of interest on Commonwealth stock had risen from £5. 5s. 0d. % in the middle of 1929 to £6. 5s. 0d. % in September 1930. In January 1931 it had risen to over £7. 10s. 0d. %. Ordinary shares had fallen in September 1930 to less than half their pre-crisis level, and were lower still in January 1931. Even bank shares had suffered a drop of 40% from the middle of 1929 to the end of 1930. Throughout 1929 bank advances had expanded, and for the fourth quarter of that year were £30 m. above the figure for the corresponding quarter of 1928. Though they were reduced in 1930, they were at the end of the year still

£16 m. above the level at the end of 1928. Deposits were,
however, falling, and the ratio of advances to deposits was
103 % in the fourth quarter of 1930, compared with 92 %
in the same quarter of 1928. This was a typical credit crisis.

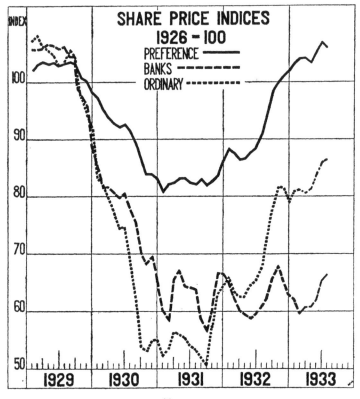

Chart 3

Values pledged against debts were collapsing, financial
institutions sought in vain to secure a reduction of outstanding debt, and the rate of interest was rising. *In industry*
the situation was not less serious. Unemployment was
rapidly rising. Official figures showed that 23 % of trade
unionists were out of work in the fourth quarter of 1930,

compared with 13% in the same quarter of 1929. These figures cannot be taken as an accurate measure of unemployment because there is some doubt as to the thoroughness of the returns. But the increasing numbers of unemployed registered with the Governments in New South Wales and Victoria and receiving sustenance showed how serious the position had become. The profits of industry had fallen rapidly. Thus for 99 companies examined, total profits in 1928/29 were £7·6 m., or 8·12% on share funds. In 1929/30 profits were £6·0 m., or 6·23% on share funds, and in 1930/31 £3·2 m., or 3·34%. The fall was specially severe in wholesale, manufacturing, retail, amusement and mining companies, and it commenced to cause grave concern to financial authorities in the latter half of 1930.[1] Here was evidence of the spreading of the loss of income. *In public finance* the year 1929/30 had closed with aggregate deficits of £11 m., and each month of the year 1930/31 showed that revenue was falling away and that an aggregate deficit of startling amount was in prospect. The banks were restive under the demands made on them for accommodation, and governments could carry on only if those demands were satisfied.

In retrospect there is nothing remarkable in this story of economic stress. During 1930 the evidence of acute disequilibrium in the economic structure accumulated with overwhelming force. But there is little in official policy to show that the country had up to the end of 1930 accepted the need for swift and drastic adjustment. It is true that in the Melbourne Agreement of August 1930, the Governments, in response to Sir Otto Niemeyer's counsel, and that of the Chairman of the Commonwealth Bank (Sir Robert Gibson), pledged themselves to balance their budgets in that year, and to refrain from uneconomic loan expenditure.

[1] These figures are from researches by Mr A. A. Fitzgerald of the University of Melbourne.

Apart from short-term credits obtained from the banks, no funds were available for loan works. Hence there was no alternative but to cut down loan expenditure, which was only £18 m. in 1930/31, compared with over £40 m. before the depression. But to balance budgets in 1930/31 was a well-nigh hopeless task from the outset, and was in any case, as will be shown later, a fundamentally unsound policy. Apart from South Australia, no Government made a satisfactory effort before the end of 1930 to reduce expenditure. Even in that State the objective seemed to recede as revenue fell away under the accumulating loss of national income. In New South Wales a beginning had been made in the task of reforming public finance, but the election in November showed with unmistakable vigour that the electorate was not convinced that the Melbourne Agreement should be honoured.

IV. *Economists' View of Loss of Income*

When one looks at the record of other countries, this hesitancy and the search after palliatives are not surprising. Democracies do not readily accept a policy of partial deflation involving reductions in some incomes and not in others. A frontal attack on wages, salaries, and government expenditure was the traditional method of dealing with such a situation. It was repulsed, and events have proved that it could not in any case have succeeded in regaining the economic position that had been lost in the crisis. The loss of income was too great, and the repercussions of that loss too disturbing, for partial and ill-considered plans to succeed in restoring balance to the economic structure.

This was evident to the economists at the time. As early as September 1930, in official advice tendered to the Acting-Commonwealth Treasurer, two of my colleagues and I drew attention to the magnitude of the task. As this memorandum was subsequently circulated, I am free to quote from it.[1] Its first two paragraphs will suffice here, but later we shall use it more freely.

(1) The sudden fall in the prices of Australian exports has reduced the value of exports by £40,000,000. An equally abrupt cessation of borrowing from overseas has caused a further loss in income from abroad of £30,000,000. The loss of income from these two sources is thus £70,000,000, more than 10 per cent. of the national income in the last year of prosperity. Unless the overseas prices of Australian exports rise, this loss is inescapable under existing conditions in Australia. It is, however, only the first loss. The reduced spending power of export producers and of those formerly dependent upon the expenditure of loan money decreases the income of workers and producers. These repercussions accentuate the loss of income and in the prevailing economic depression the total fall in national income will be of the order of double the first loss, that is, £140,000,000. This colossal sum cannot be met from a surplus of income held by a comparatively few people. It has caused serious losses of income by three sections of the community, and probably no class has completely escaped. Under existing conditions, the main burden has been borne by export producers, investors in company stocks and others dependent upon profits, and the growing numbers of unemployed.

(2) This distribution of the loss is inequitable, and the first problem of economic readjustment is to distribute the first loss of income fairly among all classes according to their capacity to bear the burden. If this condition is fulfilled, it will then be possible by a sound monetary policy to restore industry and employment, and thus to counteract the repercussions from the first loss of income, and to provide a means of escape from the indirect losses. In this way the paralysing effects of depression will be overcome and confidence in the future of industry restored. This is the second problem of economic readjustment. Under any monetary policy that may be adopted these two conditions of economic recovery must be observed. By sharing the original loss equitably among all classes and by restoring private industry, the loss of national income will be confined to the first loss. As general efficiency increases and industry absorbs the unemployed, it is probable that some of this first loss will also be made good.

[1] "A Plan for Economic Adjustment." A Memorandum prepared by D. B. Copland, L. F. Giblin and E. C. Dyason, September 18th, 1930.

The estimate of the loss of income given in the above extract was necessarily conjectural. It was an underestimate. In April 1932 the national income in 1930/31 was estimated by the Wallace Bruce Committee at £459 m. compared with £645 m. in 1928/29, a drop of £186 m.[1] The explanation is to be found in the fall in export prices after September 1930, when we made our first estimate. On the 1928 base, export prices in Australian currency had fallen from 946 in January 1929 to 638 in August 1930. They continued to fall, and were 515 in December 1930. Moreover, even short-term borrowing ceased in London in 1930, and Australia was forced to repay £14 m. of the short-term debt of £18 m. owed in August 1930 to the London money market. In these circumstances and in the absence of a comprehensive plan of adjustment, the loss of income was naturally greater even than the somewhat alarming estimate we made in September 1930.

V. *Forces Sustaining National Income*

The loss of income during the downward phase of a depression is, of course, cumulative. Until the general deflation is checked, national income must continue to fall. While this movement is in progress there is no possibility of recovery. If continued long enough, as it was in the United States, where income fell by more than 50%, widespread insolvency and financial distress must ensue. In Australia the loss of income on gold values was even greater than in the United States, for export prices fell in gold values from 1000 in 1928 to 310 for the latter half of 1932. This fall of nearly 70% in export values, together with the cessation of borrowing, would, in the absence of expansion of exports, have brought national income in gold values down by about two-thirds in the long run, for income from

---

[1] From Report quoted in Shann and Copland, *The Australian Price Structure*, p. 44.

abroad (exports and borrowing) would have fallen from £170 m. to about £45 m., i.e. £30 m. less for borrowing and some £95 m. less for exports. Even allowing for a decrease from 25% to say 20% in the ratio of overseas income to national income, the total national income would have been of the order of £220 m. compared with £650 m. before the depression. But I need not pursue this academic point here. It is sufficient to have drawn attention to the devastating effects that maintenance of the gold standard would have caused. Australia did not adhere to gold values, and her loss of national income must be considered in terms of Australian currency.

We have seen that national income fell from £645 m. in 1928/29 to £459 m. in 1930/31. For 1931/32 the estimate is £A. 430 m., giving a decrease of £A. 215 m., exactly one-third. The heavy fall took place in the years 1929/30 and 1930/31. A glance at Chart 2 shows that export prices in all currencies (Australian, sterling and gold) fell very rapidly and almost continuously during 1929 and 1930. In Australian currency the fall from January 1929 to January 1931 was 46%, while in gold and sterling it was 55%. From the 1928 level the decline at the beginning of 1931 was 49% in Australian currency and 57% in sterling. During 1931 and 1932, export prices in Australian currency fluctuated around a level 45% below the 1928 level. Had no other change taken place, national income, even in depreciated Australian currency, would have continued to fall towards a position at about one-half of its former level. This assumes a cessation of long-term borrowing overseas, and some rise in the ratio of domestic production to export production. The spreading of the loss of income from exports and borrowing would inevitably have caused a loss of the order of one-half. But other forces intervened. These forces were the increase in the volume of export production, the use of reserves to meet external obligations, the practice of withholding transfer of payments for imports in the hope of a return to exchange parity, the expansion of central bank credit to meet budget deficits and finance loan expenditure, and the traditional Australian policy of maintaining "the man on the land" through credit expansion. It is impossible to estimate the respective effects of these forces, but they all operated to check the loss of income, and towards the end of 1932 to promote some recovery. The use of exchange reserves was, of course, temporary. It was equivalent to a continuance of overseas borrowing for some time, but its effect in this direction was moderated by the maintenance of imports at too high a level during 1929/30 and 1930/31. The extension of credit for public finance and producers' maintenance held up internal spending power and the price level, and thus operated to check the fall in money income. The expansion of export production was a powerful force operating in the same direction. In 1931/32 the volume of exports was over 25 % greater than the average volume for the three pre-depression years. Exports in that year, including exports of gold from current production, were £stg. 78 m., or £A. 100.[1] With exports at the pre-depression volume, the income would have been only £A. 80 m. Bearing in mind the indirect effects of the increased spending power in the hands of export producers, the expansion of export production was of great importance in checking the fall in national income.[2] The net effect of all these forces was to limit the fall in income to one-third. In their absence the fall would have been of the order of one-half.

[1] From July to November the exchange premium was 30%, and thereafter 25%.

[2] The effect of increased volume on price must not be ignored. This cannot be estimated, but it was not great in wheat because it added little to total world wheat supplies, or in wool, because the expansion was not pronounced.

VI. *The Loss of Real Income*

Before considering the first impact of the loss of money income on different income elements, I proceed to consider the difference between the money loss and the real loss, and to attempt an estimate of the real loss. Money income may fall while real income rises. Thus in a creditor and food-importing country like Great Britain it is doubtful whether, apart from the temporary disturbances to internal investment, there has been any loss of real income during the depression.[1] If the money loss were more equitably spread over the several income elements, the disturbances of the money loss would be lessened and finally eliminated. The way would then be open for recovery. It would appear therefore that the problem of adjusting economic life to a money loss of income of the order of 15%, as in the case of Great Britain, is simple *provided the economic structure is flexible.* But in England many resistances have occurred to prevent the adjustment. Where the loss of money income is one-third, even without loss of real income, the adjustment required is much greater. But Australia suffered a severe loss of real income caused by (*a*) the cessation of borrowing overseas, and (*b*) an alteration in the terms of trade. The first needs no explanation. Its effect in causing a loss of real income was mitigated for a time by the use of exchange reserves. Later, the expansion of export production may be said to have offset to a large extent for the time being the loss from borrowing. Thus in 1931/32 Australia gained approximately £16 m. sterling from the higher volume of exports. Since we may roughly estimate the fall in import prices in sterling from 1928/29 to 1931/32 at 30%,[2] in

---

[1] I deduce this from Mr Colin Clark's estimates of British national income. See especially his article in *The Economic Journal*, June 1930.

[2] According to the Wallace Bruce Committee, import prices in Australian currency fell from 90 in 1928/29 to 82 in 1930/31. For the latter year the sterling index would be 66, giving a fall of nearly 27%. There has been a reduction since, and the suggestion of 30% is a low estimate. If so, it merely strengthens the argument that follows in the paragraph.

sterling the £30 m. of overseas borrowing before the depression could be reduced to £21 m. now and bring the same benefit in current income to Australia. For 1932/33 a preliminary estimate of the expansion of export volume over the three pre-depression years gives 30%. Australia received £83 m. sterling for exports in 1932/33. Hence the amount realised for expansion in volume was £19 m. As import prices fell still further in 1932/33, we may reckon a fall of 33⅓% in sterling prices of imports as reasonable. This will give £20 m. for 1932/33 as the sterling value of pre-depression overseas borrowing. For all practical purposes we may ignore this difference, but in doing so we must not assume the permanence of the expansion of export production as off-setting the loss of income from borrowing.

The above results might have been presented in terms of Australian currency. Since we propose to set off first the use of reserves and later the expansion of export production against the loss of overseas borrowing, it is easier to use sterling values. In considering the real loss from the altered terms of trade, it will be desirable to use Australian currency values. A simple method of stating the position is to consider the change in the terms of trade between 1928/29 and 1932/33. Export prices in Australian currency had fallen by roughly 40%, and import prices by nearly 20%. Hence the downward movement in the terms of trade is of the order of 25%. If no other force had intervened to alter the effect of a change in the terms of trade upon internal economy, this figure would be an approximate measure of the loss of national income. It is too high because the expansion of credit for governmental purposes and for maintaining primary producers acted as a stimulus to real as well as to money income. On this point consider for a moment the effect of the wheat bounty of 4½d. per bushel in 1931/32. This was paid from the issue of treasury bills by the Commonwealth Bank, that is, from the expansion of central bank credit. Had the whole sum been spent on goods by wheat farmers, there can be little doubt that for that year real income would have been increased by the payment of the bounty. Moreover, the effects would be spread into 1932/33, for the whole bounty would not be spent at once. Even if it were, the indirect effects upon the income of other producers must be considered. These effects could not have spent themselves in 1931/32. No doubt part of the bounty was used to liquidate debt, and much of this would probably not be re-invested at once by the financial institutions concerned. To this extent the bounty would not operate to expand real income. But unlike forced saving from current income, it would not have any deflationary effect on income or prices. I am not concerned here with the many other problems to which this type of credit gives rise. There can be little doubt that it checked the fall in real as well as money income.

We cannot, therefore, assume that the alteration in the terms of trade is a measure of the loss of real income. It is nevertheless the main cause of the permanent loss of real income. With a 25 % adverse movement in the terms of trade, the loss in real income must be substantial.[1] According to the method used by the Wallace Bruce Committee, the loss from 1928/29 to 1931/32 was nearly 18 %. Real income on this method is measured by adjusting the money value of national income for changes in retail prices. The Committee found the loss of real income for 1930/31 to be as much as 20 %. Production figures for 1932/33 are not available, but we know that exports were 7 % higher than in 1931/32, and that an expansion of manufacturing production had taken place. Moreover, retail prices had fallen to 26 % below their 1928/29 level, and at the end of the

[1] This would not be the case if some fundamental change had taken place in the ratio of exports to production. No doubt the ratio has fallen a little, and to this extent the effect of the less favourable terms of trade in reducing real income has been mitigated.

year 1932/33 were approximately 30% below. With a larger money income and a lower retail price level, the loss of real income in 1932/33 compared with 1928/29 would be substantially less than in either of the two previous years. The upper limit is probably 15%. With export prices on a level now 35% to 40% above their relatively stable position in 1931 and 1932, and import prices still down 20% on their pre-depression level, the loss of real income in the current year will be still further reduced. But there are no indications at present that it can be reduced below 10%, the figure suggested by economists at the beginning of the depression as being the probable permanent fall in real income on account of the crisis. In 1930 I expressed the view that "on present prospects of price movements for export production, and with a moderate programme of overseas borrowing, Australia must look forward during, say, the next five years, to a reduction of her national income of 10%".[1] Though Australia is now recovering from the heaviest loss of real income, namely that of about 20% in 1930/31, it is doubtful whether she can hope to bring the loss down to 10%. A figure somewhere between 10% and 15% is the order of real loss that has to be met unless export prices recover more rapidly than seems probable, domestic production competing with imports expands considerably, imports of capital are resumed on an unexpected scale, or new avenues of export production are successfully explored. He would be a bold man who would attempt to forecast benefits to be got from one or more of these sources. In present circumstances a lower limit of 10% real loss is somewhat optimistic. This means, it may be added, a greater real loss than 10% per head. Population has increased by about 4% since the end of 1929.

[1] *The Economic Journal*, December 1930, p. 645. I should add that the overseas borrowing contemplated is not governmental borrowing on the old lines, but private investment. This problem is discussed in Lecture VIII.

If in 1932/33 real income as a whole were 15% below the 1928/29 level, the fall in income per head would be more than 17%. When changes in population are considered, we must therefore think of a probable loss of real income per head in the immediate future of something definitely above 10%, perhaps approaching 15%.

This is important, because any further fall in internal prices will raise the level of real incomes, especially income from fixed charges, and thus militate against recovery. The theoretical and practical problems this raises must be deferred until later, when we have dealt with all aspects of the adjustments made in the crisis. A clear understanding of the magnitude of the loss, both money and real, was necessary for working out the plan of adjustment. Early in 1931, when the plan was developed and agreed upon, the real loss was probably under-estimated. This fact has an important bearing on future policy, and will be considered in later lectures.

VII. *The Early Distribution of the Money Loss*

We have seen that the greatest fall in real income was registered in 1930/31. Money income fell by nearly £30 m. in the next year, but real income was higher. How was the great loss of money income shared by different income groups in the early stages of the depression? We have to remember that the loss was cumulative over the years 1930 and 1931. If we take any point in these years it is difficult to say what the loss had been up to that time. Between September 1930 and February 1931 considerable attention was devoted to this problem by economists, who were asked to tender official advice on budgetary and other matters. At this time it was estimated that the loss of income in 1929/30 compared with 1928/29 would be of the order of £100 m. For 1930/31 a further loss of about £70 m. was suggested. In September 1930 this second loss had not occurred, but the first had. In 1929/30 the spreading effect of the direct loss caused by lower export prices and reduced borrowing had by no means been completed. The first impact only had been felt, and it was in part because this impact operated harshly on some classes that acute internal difficulties arose. The impact of the loss of income at the end of 1930 was indeed the major problem before the country. In the fourth quarter of 1930 the money loss had reached a figure of about £140 m. How was it then distributed?

Income from wages and salaries are estimated at from 50% to 55% of total national income. For 1928/29 they may be put at £350 m. of a national income of £645 m. An estimate of income from internal interest and fixed payments of all kinds, including savings bank interest, gave a figure of £80 m.[1] Income from ordinary shares was estimated at £30 m., and professional income at £20 m. This left £165 m. as income from land production and from trade and manufactures not already included in the above figures. This is strictly speaking entrepreneur income, if we include in this income the wages of owner-managers working on a small scale, and the profits of private businesses. This estimate is admittedly rough, but the margin of possible error is not sufficiently great to invalidate the argument based upon it.

We have, therefore, for 1928/29 a classification of income on the following lines:

	£ m.
Wages and salaries	350
Interest and fixed payments ...	80
Ordinary shares	30
Professional	20
Entrepreneur	165
	645

[1] We know income from bank interest and bond interest. Estimates of interest from preference shares and mortgage interest and rents are made on the basis of capital values.

It will be observed that the income from fixed charges was about 12·5 % of total income. This was not, however, the total burden of fixed payments upon the Australian economy. We are considering here only internal income, but if we include outgoings for external interest and sinking fund (public and private) we have to add £36 m. to the fixed charges, bringing them up to £116 m. This is nearly 18 % of total national income. By the end of 1930 this class of income was being hit by the depression because some debtors were unable to pay all their interest, but the repercussions had not been as serious as on other classes. An all-round reduction of 10 % would be a reasonable estimate. Later, the loss was greater even before the last half of 1931, when the interest and rent reductions were made. On income from wages and salaries few statutory reductions had been made, but the increase in unemployment and the reductions in salaries suggested a loss of at least 12½ %. For ordinary shares, investigations showed that a fall of 20 % had been realised in 1929/30. As profits were falling very rapidly in 1930 the loss must have been one-third by the end of the year. Professional income had also suffered, probably to the extent of 25 %. How was entrepreneur income affected? Some elements in it would be relatively stable, e.g. fixed charges on volume of goods handled, income from protected agricultural products with little export surplus, and income from sheltered services not greatly reduced at first by the depression. In the main, however, this income was exposed to the full blast of the depression. It bore at first the main brunt of the fall in export prices, and was immediately affected by the drop in loan expenditure, and the rapid reduction in volume of production in protected and sheltered industry. Entrepreneur income would be reduced by at least three-quarters of the direct loss of income from exports. Inasmuch as this loss operated over all export production, and not merely on exports, it is reasonable to suppose that entrepreneur income would be reduced to the full extent of the loss of export income. This was approximately £50 m. by the end of 1930.[1] To this must be added losses on account of reduced commission on commercial transactions and reductions in manufacturing output. The fall in prices and the contraction in manufacturing production was thought to be sufficient at the end of 1930 to increase the losses on entrepreneur income to £80 m., or approximately 47% of that income in 1928/29.

The estimated losses of the several classes of income at the end of 1930 were then as follows:

	Loss of income	
	%	£ m.
Wages and salaries... ...	12·5	43
Interest and fixed payments	10·0	8
Ordinary shares	33·3	10
Professional	25·0	5
Entrepreneur	47·0	80
		146

This was roughly the position at the end of 1930. In the first stages of the crisis the impact fell upon income from ordinary shares and entrepreneur income. Losses to wages and salary earners and professional men quickly followed, but they were not proportional to the losses of the first two classes affected. Interest and fixed charges would be the last and the least severely hit. In respect of real income, wage earners had not suffered as a whole up to the end of 1930. Real income from interest and fixed charges had actually increased, but there had been a reduction of real income in all other classes, especially in entrepreneur income.

---

[1] This is £50 m. in Australian currency at a time when this currency was depreciated by only 8% compared with 23% in February 1931.

These inequalities in money and real losses of income were much more marked in the early stages of the crisis. I have endeavoured to give you a picture of the position as we saw it about the end of 1930. The losses of income were far in excess of what was generally realised, and economists put forward estimates of heavy losses with some hesitancy. When we first drew attention to the unequal loss of income early in 1930, the inequalities were even more glaring, though total losses had not been as great. What followed in economic policy was largely determined by this inequality of impact, as well as by the total loss of income. The development of the idea that the control of the impact of the loss of income was the way out of the depression is the theme of the next lecture.

III

ALTERNATIVE METHODS OF ADJUST-MENT—THE ECONOMISTS' PLAN

I. *The Fallacy of Early Policy*

IN the period of expediency from the middle of 1929 to early in 1931, official attention was focused upon Australia's external or transfer problem. Australia sought to meet her obligations without a fundamental change of internal policy. Overseas authorities sought to prevent any internal development that might encourage Australia to pursue an unorthodox financial or economic policy. In so far as any policy was suggested from outside authorities, it was a policy of balancing the budget, reducing salaries and wages, and maintaining the gold standard. Internally Australia had no policy. She adopted a series of expedients to meet the transfer difficulty. To the extent that she acted on the internal position her action was largely inconsistent with her desire to handle successfully her transfer problem.

The expedients were mentioned in Lecture II. They may, for convenience, again be summarised here:

(1) Export of gold and use of exchange reserves.

(2) Higher tariff duties and import restrictions and prohibitions.

(3) A pegged exchange over-valuing the currency.

(4) An exchange pool to guarantee the service on the external debt.

Let us consider this series of makeshifts. It was proper to use reserves in a crisis. What is a reserve for if not to be used in times of difficulty? Unlike some central banks which seem to think that a reserve is an immovable object,

Australia quickly made her reserves liquid; so quickly indeed that the gold of the private banks began to run off at rates equal to or near parity when it might have commanded a considerable premium. But the banks, with one important exception, were against any currency depreciation, and throughout 1930 they sought as far as possible to hold Australian currency above its real value. Thus exchange reserves were freely used throughout 1929 and 1930 without any serious action being taken to remove the conditions necessitating their use, namely, a heavy unfavourable balance of payments on income account. The Government stepped in with its tariff weapon. Unlike currency depreciation, this weapon offers no help to export production, but rather hampers it, and operates unevenly upon imports and local production. It adds to costs without relieving export producers, and shelters protected industries from the competition of more efficient producers. It provides no general correction for distortions in the price structure, but on the contrary rather aggravates already existing distortions. Australia already had an uneconomic tariff, and the new tariff was mainly an imposition of still higher protection in the guise of a method of adjusting the balance of payments. But as I have written elsewhere, the tariff is a kind of one-way elastic and cannot be contracted.[1] How far the tariff was effective in reducing imports will always be a disputed point. That imports could have been brought down without heavy increases in tariffs cannot be disputed. Currency depreciation and earlier contraction of credit by the banks would have speedily brought satisfactory results. This action, moreover, would have promoted other desirable lines of action calculated to expedite recovery. The increase in the tariff was unnecessary; it retarded speedy adjustment, and is to-day one of the most

[1] *What Have the Banks Done?* (Angus and Robertson, Sydney), 1931, p. 23.

important serious hindrances to complete recovery because it helps to sustain a distorted price structure.[1]

The formation in 1930 of an exchange pool through which the Government was guaranteed £3 m. per month for meeting external commitments was the inevitable outcome of previous policy. With the currency over-valued at the banks' carded rate of £A. 106. 10s. 0d. for £stg. 100, and surplus exchange reserves running out, it was doubtless necessary to give the Government first call on current funds in London. By this time the banks were thoroughly alive to the need of restricting imports. They did this through the traditional policy of rationing credits to importers, but they were still on the whole desirous of keeping the currency as close to parity with gold as possible. By doing so they increased their own difficulties in keeping down imports, and prevented exporters from securing much-needed relief from the depreciation of the currency. Fortunately, there was no compulsory pooling of current London funds received from exports. This enabled the "open" or "black" market in exchange to flourish. In this market London funds could be sold at a premium that ultimately rose to double the bank premium.[2] In the end the "black" market won, but it was not until January 1931 that the banks again took command of the market.

It would appear that both government and bank opinion in the early stages of the crisis favoured this attempt to deal with the crisis as primarily a transfer problem. In fairness to the banks, however, it ought to be stated that they pressed for reductions in wages and government expenditure. In this they were very strongly supported by Sir Otto Nie-

---

[1] Australia got her heavy increases in the tariff when the protected industries wanted shelter from the economic storm brewing abroad. They were not required because with currency depreciation and cuts in costs later adopted, her costs fell relative to external costs. If Australia acted unwisely by increasing her tariff, what shall we say of Great Britain? Tariffs were imposed after the depreciation of the currency, when they were least needed.

[2] Later developments in exchange policy are discussed in Lecture V.

meyer, who met the Loan Council at an historic meeting in August 1930. But up to the end of 1930 internal adjustments consistent with "transfer" policy had not proceeded far. Nor was there any clear grasp, among even those who favoured drastic deflation, of the magnitude of the task before them. At the moment consumers' income at home was in effect being held up by extensions of credit to governments and to primary producers, while it was being pressed down by an over-valued currency giving lower and lower prices to primary producers.[1] The fundamental error of this policy was bound to emerge quickly. With the progress of deflation abroad and the decline in consumers' income at home, government revenue began to slump seriously, output in protected and sheltered industries to decline, unemployment to increase, and the profits of industry to disappear. Added to this was an increasing lack of confidence in the capacity of governments to handle a difficult situation.

I need not weary you with details of the theoretical argument that shows the inconsistency of attempts to overvalue a currency and at the same time avoid internal deflation. A classic statement of the problem is to be found in Mr Hawtrey's *Currency and Credit*, Chap. v.[2] We need only substitute a fall in export prices for Mr Hawtrey's "failure of the harvest" to show that a heavy reduction in local currency values of income from export production must be followed by a deflation of all other income. The greater the relative importance of export income to total income, the greater the pressure for the deflation of internal income. The propping up of the Australian price level and income by high export prices and heavy overseas borrowing

[1] Governments had received credits from the Commonwealth Bank of £18·2 m. at June 1930 and £30·3 m. at December 1930. For the fourth quarter of 1930 bank advances were £270 m. compared with £255 m. in the fourth quarter of 1928.

[2] See also Keynes, *Treatise on Money*, Vol. I, Chap. 21.

in the period 1925 to 1929 gives Mr Hawtrey's argument added weight when applied to Australia in 1930. Parity with sterling had been possible under the easy conditions operating immediately prior to the depression. To make it a cardinal feature of depression policy was a fundamental mistake.

II. *The Policy of Deflation*

This mistake was common to the policy proposed by the advocates of the two schools of thought that emerged in the latter half of 1930. By this time internal difficulties were increasing, and it was necessary to evolve some plan of internal economic adjustment to the new conditions imposed by the depression. We shall specify these two schools of thought as deflationist and inflationist respectively. There was really a third that became vocal in the so-called Lang Plan. It was silent on the question of currency depreciation and was violently inflationist except in respect of income from interest, which it would control rigorously and reduce severely. For the most part the deflationists were also illogical in their treatment of interest and fixed charges generally. They held that interest would fall over a period and were content to apply a deliberate deflationist policy to all other income elements.

We proceed to examine the theory of deflation as applied to the Australian economy at the end of 1930. At that time the loss of income was of the order of £140 m., or more than 20% below the 1928/29 level. But this school accepted parity with sterling as its fundamental monetary principle. It would certainly endorse Sir Otto Niemeyer's maxim that "rising exchange rates prejudice the whole fabric of national finance". (Statement before the Premiers' Conference in August 1930.) Australia was at the time off the sterling standard by about 6% according to the bank rate. Early in 1931 the currency was at a discount of 23%. Hence the loss

of money income to be considered was much more than
£140 m., though the exponents of deflation had perhaps
not realised that it was even as much as this figure. For
the year 1930/31 national income in the depreciated
Australian currency had fallen over £180 m. below the
1928/29 level. In sterling values the fall would be not less
than £245 m. on 1928/29 standards.[1] The loss of income
would then be of the order of 37%. With the further fall of
export prices in sterling in 1931/32 and with no expansion
of central bank credit, the ultimate loss in sterling values
would have approached 50%.[2] A loss of this magnitude
was perhaps not foreseen even by the critics of this school.
Nevertheless, they agreed that the loss was so severe as to
render escape from depression by deflation an impossible
task. Assuming for the moment a loss of 40% in money
income, let us consider some of the effects of deflation:

(1) Since real income, as argued in Lecture II, would
have fallen by at least 10%, the reduction in money wages
required by deflation would have been of the order of 50%.
This clearly was impossible over a short period.

(2) Allowing for a "natural" fall[3] of 20% in internal
interest and fixed charges, these would have been £64 m.,
while external interest and sinking fund would have been
reduced from £36 m. to about £27 m.[4] The total would
be £91 m., or 23% of national income, compared with
18% before the depression.

---

[1] This assumes a reduction of 12½% only in money income for 1930/31,
bringing it down from £A. 459 m. to about £stg. 400 m.

[2] This loss would have been reduced if borrowing in London could have
been resumed as the adherents of deflation confidently anticipated.

[3] With characteristic force Professor Cannan has stated the method by
which this would be accomplished. "So-called 'fixed-interest' should be
allowed to be eaten away by defaults and stoppages without too much
attention being given to the injustices involved." (*The Economic Journal*,
September 1932, p. 370.)

[4] This allows £5·5 m. saving through the war debt concession, £1·5 m.
from conversions, and £2 m. reduction of private interest and other sterling
payments.

(3) The budget position would have been alarming. In 1929/30 expenditure of the seven governments was approximately £180 m., of which about one-third was for interest and sinking fund on debt. We can allow £7 m. reduction of this on account of interest savings overseas, and another £3 m. for reduction in special sinking fund payments and other possible savings. Against this saving must be set provision for unemployment, which would have been exceedingly high under undiluted deflation. This would be at least £10 m. We are left with £120 m. of expenditure on which to make savings. With a fall in income of 40%, government revenue would decline by at least one-third, or over £60 m. Hence it would have been necessary to reduce ordinary government expenditure by this sum on a total of £120 m., that is, by about 50%. If it is contended that increases in taxation would have been possible, my reply is that a deficit of nearly £10 m. was incurred in 1929/30. Any new taxation possible on the lower income would have been necessary to meet this deficit. The Melbourne Agreement of August 1930, based on the policy of deflation, contemplated an immediate balancing of the budget. Even on the modest assumption of an ultimate loss of $33\frac{1}{3}$% of revenue, very low in the circumstances, no one can confidently assert that budget balancing by deflation alone was practicable.

(4) How would the export trades have fared? Wool would have realised less than 7*d.* per lb., and wheat about 2*s.* 4*d.* per bushel. These are sea-board prices, and are below costs of production, even with the lower costs possible under deflation. Export production could not have been sustained on these prices without great remissions in interest and debt, and assistance from financial institutions. Little or no expansion of export production could have taken place under these conditions.

(5) The sterling value of exports would have been about

£65 m. instead of over £80 m. To meet overseas interest, imports of less than £40 m. would be permissible. This would be modified by borrowing, but only temporary relief could be got from this source. The external debt structure would have become intolerable.

(6) Finally, the whole basis of internal credit would have been undermined. The fall in values of all securities would have been such as to imperil the solvency of all financial institutions, including banks, savings banks and insurance companies. This was a point that, by some curious mental lapse, seemed to have escaped the notice of deflationists. Perhaps their under-estimate of the extent to which it would have been necessary to pursue deflation was responsible for failure to note this grave defect in their policy.

This is a formidable array of difficulties in the way of a successful deflation policy. To those who believe in the "cleansing crisis", with its wholesale insolvency and writing down of debt, deflation probably has no terrors. I am unable to follow even their theory, because the frictional elements are so great, even in a flexible economic structure, as to prevent a rapid and comprehensive application of deflation. For a long time real wages would be higher than before the crisis, the real rate of interest would also be higher, and an acute shortage of working capital would be experienced. Since the demand for the factors of production, especially labour and capital, is elastic, higher real wages and real rates of interest would retard recovery. The money loss of national income would be needlessly heavy, and the level of unemployment needlessly high. In the end an expansion of credit to provide working capital would be necessary. This would reduce rates of interest, raise prices and reduce real wages. Deflation is regarded perhaps as a preparation for this initial positive step to recovery. The Australian aboriginals have a terrible initiation ceremony before the young man assumes the status of manhood. But they also have a tradition of stoic endurance to the pain and distress of initiation, and special rewards for capacity to endure exceptionally severe treatment. The Australian democracy has proved its capacity to endure much, but neither it nor any other democracy would pass through the initiation ceremony required by deflation when it knows that the ceremony is itself unnecessary. Let these ceremonies continue where superstition still controls society, but in a supposedly enlightened age people rightly reject a policy that involves needless disorganisation and distress. In the memorandum from which I quoted in the last lecture, we rejected deflation on the following ground, among others: "If the deflation of the price level necessary to restore exchange parity could be accomplished over 20 years, the depressing effects upon industry would be small, and severe unemployment could be avoided. But the task of reducing prices rapidly cannot be accomplished without a substantial increase in the present numbers of unemployed. This is the worst aspect of hasty deflation, but it is by no means the only serious objection to such a policy".

III. *Inflation Proposals*

At the other end of the scale were those who believed in a policy of inflation as the way out for Australia. This policy, as I have said already, was to be pursued without heavy depreciation of the currency. Thus the Hon. E. G. Theodore, in his memorandum of March 1931 to members of the Federal Parliamentary Labour Party, explaining the Commonwealth Government's monetary proposals for restoring the price level of 1925 to 1929, stated that it was intended "that the exchange rate should be allowed to go to a level commensurate with the disparity in the Australian price levels as compared with those overseas". The exchange rate was then £A. 130 to £stg. 100, and this would have been sufficient to meet Mr Theodore's condition. He

added, however, that the Exchange Mobilisation Scheme
(the exchange pool already mentioned) would be continued
and if necessary "a greater control will be assumed under
the powers contained in the Customs Act, which would
permit the prohibition of all exports except under licence".
The specific proposal enunciated by Mr Theodore was the
issue of £18 m. fiduciary notes, of which £6 m. was to be
used to pay a bounty of 6*d.* per bushel on wheat, and £12 m.
for absorbing unemployed on "useful and productive
work". Other elements included in the programme were
drastic reorganisation of banking, including (*a*) amendments to the Commonwealth Bank Act to give the Government "greater power and authority in supply and control
of public credit and in control of interest rates" and to
eliminate the 25% obligatory gold reserve against notes,
(*b*) the creation of an independent central bank, and (*c*) a
bill for controlling interest and discount rates. I have
examined this programme in detail elsewhere,[1] and do not
intend to weary you with a detailed account of what was
a passing political phase. I select Mr Theodore's proposals
as being a considered and constructive plan for escape from
depression through inflation.

We can concede the argument of the inflationists that
"a campaign of economy alone, no matter how drastic,
would be inadequate to bring about budget equilibrium".[2]
But this did not establish the case for inflation alone as a
means of attaining budget equilibrium and general economic equilibrium. There was at the moment a strong and
determined political resistance to governmental economies
in both the Commonwealth and the New South Wales

[1] Monthly Summary of National Bank of Australasia, April 1931, reprinted in Shann and Copland, *The Battle of the Plans* (Angus and Robertson,
Sydney), pp. 20–29. This book also contains Mr Theodore's memorandum
referred to above, his correspondence with the Commonwealth Bank, and
a circular of the Bank of New South Wales, all apposite to the problem.

[2] Mr Theodore's letter of April 15th, 1931, to Sir Robert Gibson, quoted
in Shann and Copland, *The Battle of the Plans*, p. 52.

Parliaments. Minor economies had been made, amounting in the case of the Commonwealth to some £2·3 m. on an expenditure of nearly £70 m. The budgetary position, as we shall see in Lecture VI, was becoming daily more serious. In the absence of a restoration of export income and drastic economies in public expenditure, the deficits in the budget would have been between £30 m. and £40 m., with no prospect of reduction in the immediate future. It is true that the expenditure of £18 m. on wheat bounty and public works would have checked the fall in income and in government revenue. But it was not a permanent solution of the budget problem or the general economic problem.

IV. *Costs and Prices under Inflation*

Consider the latter first. Export prices in Australian currency had fallen at that time by 45% to 50% on the pre-depression level. There was no plan for raising these prices or for increasing income from exports, apart from the £6 m. proposed wheat bounty. For some years before the crisis, exports were on the average about 22% of national income. In the absence of overseas borrowing they would be higher, perhaps 25%, unless workers displaced by contraction of public works found profitable employment in industry competing with imports and in sheltered industry. But this could not happen under inflation (and pegged exchange rates) because local costs would remain high while overseas costs were falling. Hence in the absence of other forces such as the permanent expenditure on public works by inflationary finance, national income would be determined largely by the money value of export income. Without a recovery in export income, a permanent recovery of national income was impossible. This was a fatal flaw in the logic of the inflationists.

A rough measure of changes in producers' costs is given by the retail price index. On the inflation plan no fall in internal prices was contemplated. At the beginning of 1931, retail prices had fallen by 20 % on the 1928 level, and to this extent producers' costs had also been reduced. The reduction in costs operated unevenly throughout industry, according to the ratio of fixed costs to adjustable costs. But the fall in retail prices may be taken as an indication of the decline in costs then in progress. Export prices in Australian currency had, however, at this time fallen by 40 % to 45 %, and were to fall still further. This meant that real costs to exporters, measured in terms of their own prices, had risen from 30 % to 40 %. To restore internal prices by inflation without restoring export prices would have caused a rise in real costs to exporters during the depression, of about 70 %. If overseas prices fell and increased the disparity between Australian and overseas prices to 40 %, the exchange rate might have risen to £A. 140 for £stg. 100. In this event export prices in Australian currency would have risen in the proportion of 130 to 140, that is, by roughly 8 %. But at this level the reduction on the 1928 standard would still have been from 35 % to 40 %, and the increase in real costs to exporters of the order of 60 %. Clearly this policy offered no solution of the exporters' difficulties.

The inflationists erred, as many before and since have erred, in concentrating on the wrong price level. Economists ought to use the term "price level" with more care and precision. What was needed in Australia in 1931, as in 1933, was a rise in export prices. A general policy of credit expansion on the lines proposed by the inflationists in 1931 would have raised the wrong price level, namely, the prices of consumers' goods generally. In doing so the policy would have increased the distortion in the price structure and increased the difficulties of export producers. The currency would have remained over-valued, for it is the relation between export producers' costs and prices that ultimately determines the relative value of a currency.

Currency depreciation is required mainly for the purpose of restoring balance between costs and prices in export production. On the inflation policy proposed, the disparity between export producers' costs and prices would have increased, as we have already seen.

V. *Inflation and the Budget*

There were other serious defects in the argument of the inflationists. Budget equilibrium could not have been attained by this method. This follows from the failure of inflation as proposed to restore permanently the money value of national income. True, government revenue would have been partially restored by the additional expenditure proposed, but in the absence of a substantial rise in export income or drastic economies in expenditure, the budget deficit would have been heavy, with no prospect of reducing it below the limit fixed by the recovery in revenue. To finance this deficit, additional credit would have been required. This could come only from the traditional method of inflation to cover deficits, and there was no reason to suppose that anything but the traditional effects on the currency would have ensued. As Lord D'Abernon has pointed out in the case of the German inflation the authorities might well suppose that the external value of the currency would not be affected in such circumstances.[1] With an uncontrolled deficit and increasing issues of treasury bills for deficits, there is no doubt that the Australian pound would have suffered the fate of the currencies of all countries that have practised this method of public finance. This was the view taken by Australian economists at the time. To quote from the report of the Committee of Under-Treasurers and Economists to the Sub-Committee of the Loan Council in May 1931. Speaking of inflation as a method of bridging the gap in the budget

[1] Quoted in Shann and Copland, *The Crisis in Australian Finance*, p. x.

and exacting a contribution from bond-holders, the Committee stated: "There can be little doubt that under present conditions such a policy would destroy confidence in the currency. With such loss of confidence both interest and exchange rates would rise. The rise in exchange would increase the cost of meeting overseas interest obligations and therefore upset the whole plan for budget equilibrium. The increase in interest rates would be damaging to conversion operations and again impose an additional strain upon the budget. The net effect would be to increase the deficit and to require an increasing amount of new credit and currency to be created for balancing the budgets in successive years. In these circumstances an inflationary policy would soon get out of hand and bring about a collapse of the currency".[1]

We thus had prospects of budget disequilibrium, heavy currency depreciation and high interest rates. The desire of the inflationists to control and reduce interest rates and to limit the depreciation of the currency was inconsistent with their proposals. It is not suggested that inflation and currency depreciation on the post-war European scale would have occurred. There were ample reasons for fearing a sufficient movement in this direction to cause grave financial disorder and delay the programme of recovery.[2] I readily admit that some further depreciation of the currency as part of a considered plan would have brought beneficial results at that time, but any proposal that could not offer a fall in long-term interest rates had little merit as a contribution to recovery. Mr Keynes has no doubt long since convinced you all in Cambridge that low long-

[1] From Report of Committee published in *Proceedings of the Premiers' Conference*, May/June 1931. Quoted in Shann and Copland, *ibid.* p. 93. Following the usual practice we shall call this Committee "the Copland Committee".

[2] A fall in bond prices would have operated very unfavourably on the banking structure, for at that time most of the assets of the Commonwealth Bank were government securities.

term interest rates are a *sine qua non* of recovery and I need not labour this point.

There was one more flaw in the logic of the inflationists. Mr Theodore spoke of "useful and productive work" as a means for restoring employment. We shall not stop to define "useful" or "productive", or to answer the critic of public works who delights to apply the rules of accountancy to loan expenditure. With our Australian experience before me I must confess that my sympathies are to a large extent with the critics.[1] In a depression there is much to be said for relaxing financial standards to provide temporary work for unemployed pending recovery. But Australia had a special problem in her public works expenditure. She had been spending £40 m. to £45 m. per annum before the depression, and she could not look forward to a resumption of loan expenditure on this scale. She had therefore to provide other "useful and productive work" for workers that would be permanently displaced by a reduction in capital expenditure. This structural change was inevitable in any case, but the depression forced it upon the country as a major adjustment. At the end of an era of great constructional expenditure, additional employment must be found in export industries or in industries competing with imports. This is the only way to replace the loss of national income caused by reduced borrowing. We had, as it were, in Australia expanded our capital equipment, and the next step was to use this equipment by increasing current output. With low export prices, high costs, and falling import prices, the necessary expansion could not have taken place in either export industry or protected industry. The "useful and productive work" would merely have added to capital equipment, while the high costs and high rates of interest

[1] Consider the case of Victoria, with probably a better record than other States. Mr F. W. Eggleston has shown in his admirable study of *State Socialism in Victoria* (King) that in 1929 the deficits in four State enterprises were £2 m. This is the deficiency in interest payments.

would have reduced the capital value of all existing capital equipment. In other words, the unfavourable conditions that emerge at the end of a boom would have been sustained and aggravated for a time only to force a later and more difficult crisis.

VI. *The Middle Course*

The arguments advanced here against these two main alternatives of deflation and inflation were in the main stated at the time.[1] Though economists rejected both the deflationist and inflationist schemes as complete and satisfactory methods of economic adjustment, they recognised at the outset that any plan for speedy adjustment must be a judicious mixture of inflation and deflation. This can be observed in the manifestos[2] they issued during the crisis, and in the report of the Under-Treasurers and Economists upon which the Premiers' Plan was based. As I cannot pretend to speak for my colleagues I shall give my own prognosis of the situation.

The central problem was the loss of national income. There was a real loss estimated at the outset to be not less than 10%, and to this extent a reduction in the standard of living was inevitable. The money loss would be determined in part by the currency policy pursued. It was essential to keep it as low as possible, and to spread it equitably and rapidly over all income elements. The smaller the money loss, the easier and more practicable would be

[1] My own objections are given in a paper on "Economic Readjustment and Currency Policy" read before the Victorian Branch of the Economic Society in June 1930 and published as Chapter 6 of *Credit and Currency Control* (Melbourne University Press), 1930. See also *The Economic Record* for November 1930, article on "Restoration of Economic Equilibrium" by Professors Giblin and Wood and myself, and the Memorandum on "A Plan for Economic Readjustment", referred to in Lecture II.

[2] There were three manifestos. The first was issued in June 1930 and the second in January 1931, and are reprinted in Shann and Copland, *The Crisis in Australian Finance* 1929–31 (Angus and Robertson). The third was issued in November 1931 and is reprinted in Shann and Copland, *The Australian Price Structure*, 1932 (Angus and Robertson).

the task of economic adjustment. The more equitably the loss was spread, the less would be the disequilibrium in the cost and price structure. Any income element, such as fixed charges, that secured a real gain in the crisis would be a barrier to recovery. "Equality of sacrifice" became a watchword later in the crisis and was the slogan adopted to popularise the Premiers' Plan. It was essentially a sound economic principle. Export production suffered most heavily in the early stages of the crisis and had to be preserved at all costs. To preserve it a shifting of the burdens of the depression from the shoulders of export producers to other shoulders was a first condition. What other shoulders? Not any in particular, but all. The exporters' burdens were their costs. Upon these costs were built up all other incomes. Hence some exaction from all incomes was required to reduce exporters' real costs. This exaction could be made either by increasing exporters' income at the expense of other incomes, or by direct reduction of other incomes, or by a judicious mixture of both. This judicious mixture became the middle course which I and others suggested in 1930.[1]

Having established the principle that the distribution of the loss of income was the fundamental condition of recovery, each element of the middle course proposed had to meet this simple test. This middle course as conceived in 1930 was based on a general reduction in real income of 10%, and as small a fall in money income as was practicable under monetary and budgetary policy. Its details were as follows:

(1) A depreciation of the currency sufficient to restore real income in export industries to 10% of its former level.

(2) A reduction in real wages of 10%.

(3) A general reduction in real government salaries and wages and expenditure of 10%.

---

[1] See in particular *Credit and Currency Control*, pp. 136–42.

(4) A super-tax of 10% on income from property.

(5) An expansionist monetary policy based upon the purchase of Government securities by the Commonwealth Bank with a view to maintaining the general level of prices as measured by the *complete* retail index number.[1]

In retrospect two criticisms of this policy may be made. First, it was impossible to sustain internal prices, as defined, without a much greater rise in exchange than was perhaps prudent at the time. In the Memorandum of September 1930, 20% was suggested "as the maximum rate required and further consideration should be given to the exact figure". The rate rose to 30% on sterling in January 1931, and to 80% on gold at the end of 1932. The Wallace Bruce Committee, composed of four economists and two business men, appointed in April 1932 to make a Preliminary Survey of the Economic Problem for a Premiers' Conference suggested as an element in "a middle course" between continued deflation and further depreciation of the currency, an increase in the exchange rate, which was then 25% on sterling and 62% on gold.[2] With sterling off gold, an exchange rate as high as 80% on gold did not occasion any alarm. A rate of 50% on sterling would, however, have caused misgivings, and the continued fall in export prices in the season 1930/31 would have required a rate of this magnitude to have made successful "the middle course" on the lines suggested above. The second criticism relates to the suggested super-tax on income from property. This could not reduce fixed charges, but might actually have increased them, though it would exact a contribution from this income element. Later, when the economic and

---

[1] This included clothing and miscellaneous expenditure in addition to food, groceries and house rent covered by the index used by the Arbitration Court for adjusting wages.

[2] This report is reproduced in Shann and Copland, *The Australian Price Structure*.

budgetary situation had become much more serious, a direct reduction of interest was suggested.[1]

VII. *The Memorandum of September* 1930

The middle course on the above lines was suggested in the Memorandum of September 1930 submitted to the Treasurer by Professor L. F. Giblin, Mr E. C. Dyason and myself. The general economic argument for the middle course as urged by three economists at the time is set out in that Memorandum. I quote the relevant section:

C. THE EFFECTS OF THE POLICY.

We may call the above policy one of stabilisation in contrast to the traditional policy of deflation discussed in Section A. We have to consider briefly the effects of the policy of stabilisation on the following:

1. Export industries.
2. Other industries.
3. Unemployment and the wage-earner.
4. Distribution of loss.
5. Government budgets.
6. Local bond-holder, interest rates and conversions.
7. Oversea bond-holders and the short loan position.

1. *Export Industries.* The ultimate effect of the two policies on cost of production will not be very different except in respect to the fixed charges of rent and interest. These are very heavy in the export industries, and with deflation would be drastically increased so as to be a crushing burden on industry; while stabilisation will not add to them. Even more important is the immediate relief given to export industry by a high exchange premium, while the effects of deflation in reducing costs will be slow and irregular. Time is the essence of the contract and delay in giving relief will cause the loss of a considerable amount of marginal production. This loss will be avoided under stabilisation, and the exchange bounty may on the contrary increase the volume of exports, not perhaps in wool and wheat, but in meat, coal, gold, base metals, hides, butter and even a number of manufactures.

---

[1] Report of the Copland Committee, May 1931.

2. *Other Industries.* The resulting increase in money income in export production will give a fillip to protected and sheltered industries and reverse the present drift to reduced output. Protected production, insofar as it is dependent upon imported raw materials, will experience increased costs on account of the higher exchange rate. But it will have relief in the reduced wage rate, and any discrepancy between this relief and the added cost of raw material can be met by a rise in prices behind the higher shelter of exchange rates. On the whole protected industry should be able to compete more effectively with imports and thus to expand. Sheltered production will experience a benefit from lower wage rates and from the added spending power of export industries. Inasmuch as the general price level remains stable, or rises only a little at first, sheltered industries should secure a net benefit and their former output should be restored. All these industries will also obtain a comparative advantage from the stabilisation of the real burden of fixed interest payments.

3. *Unemployment and the Wage-Earner.* Provided both essential parts of the policy, i.e., a reduction in real wages and a stable money system are carried out, we should expect unemployment to decrease gradually, but we would not expect any sudden change. Complete recovery might require two or three years even under the best conditions, but under a rapid deflationary policy—we see no escape from increasing unemployment which would become desperately serious as the means to ameliorate it became exhausted. The policy of stabilisation requires only one cut in wages, in contrast with the cumulative reductions required under a deflationary policy. The reduction in real wages may be the same in both cases, but the practical difficulties of securing it without grave industrial trouble are vastly greater in the one case than in the other.

4. *The Distribution of Loss.* Under stabilisation with a super-tax on income from property the loss of national income is equitably distributed. Deflation would give to the recipients of rent and interest and all fixed payments a continually higher real income and a constantly increasing share of the products of industry.

5. *Government Budgets.* We have suggested a reduction in government expenditure and this is being achieved in some States. The fall in revenue is, however, so serious that no practicable reduction in expenditure can relieve the budget sufficiently. The main cause of budget deficits is a languishing

revenue and this cause cannot be removed until industry is restored and the fall in national income checked. As indicated above this process of restoration will take place more rapidly under stabilisation than under deflation, and we look forward to an automatic increase in revenue under the former policy.

This consideration outweighs all others, but there are some sources of revenue that require brief discussion. If the exchange rate was 20%, the customs duties under such conditions would be automatically increased by this amount. Assuming a revenue from customs, apart from excise, of £20 m. (at parity of exchange) the customs revenue would benefit to the extent of £4 m., by a policy of stabilisation. In addition to this, the actual volume of exports will be substantially increased, in comparison to what exports would be (if parity were restored) during the period of deflation of costs. It is impossible to estimate this difference, but it may well be of the order of £10 m. at overseas prices, and mean an addition (because of the increased imports) in customs revenue in Australian currency, at 20% discount, of £3 m., making a total increase possibly £7 m. of revenue compared with parity of exchange.

Against this must be set the amount of increased exchange payable on Government remittances abroad on a 20% exchange. This increase on Commonwealth and State remittances will amount to £6 m. in Australian currency above that at parity. The increased revenue from customs would make it possible to pay the whole of this exchange premium on behalf of both Commonwealth and States, and still have a substantial surplus compared with the position at parity of exchange.

The increase in revenue due to the quicker restoration of national prosperity referred to above would bring considerably larger returns from income tax and excise, and prompter payment of all direct taxes. In addition, the financial position of the States in respect to income tax, railway receipts, etc., would be considerably improved under a stabilisation policy.

6. *The Effect on the Local Bond-holder, Interest Rates and Conversions.* Decreasing prices benefit the holder of all money claims and increasing prices damage him. Provided the financial fabric holds and doubts as to the ability of Governments to meet their obligations are removed, conversions will be more easily arranged and at lower rates while the deflationary process is going on, but this advantage is at the expense of paralysis of industry and great unemployment. The market operations suggested under the policy will ease the

difficulties of the present situation and, we think, with the greater confidence engendered, will, on balance, cause some easing of interest rates and facilitate conversions. But we cannot too strongly emphasise that suggestions of wholesale inflation will utterly destroy the chance of conversions, except on the most extravagant terms.

7. *The Effect on Overseas Bond-holders and the Present Short Loan Position.* The effects of a 20% exchange rate on the London Money Market will be somewhat unfavourable but if, when the change is made, the Commonwealth Bank management were to announce that pending internal readjustment, the exchange rate had been increased for the purpose of sustaining the export industries and so making it possible for the country to meet its external obligations, then the effects would not, so far as our judgment on this matter goes, be serious. But again, it is essential that the assurance be given that the situation will be under control. The position of the external bond-holder is not affected in any way by such an internal adjustment, provided it is clear that internal real costs are to be reduced and industry maintained. We think, however, that the alteration in the exchange rate should be made immediately, so as to be an accepted fact well before the next approach to the London market.

In conclusion, we emphasise the urgency of immediate action on the lines suggested. The mechanism of industry is still intact and we believe it is possible by these adjustments to restore it to its normal capacity. A continuance of the present drift threatens the fabric of industry with damage that could only be repaired at a sacrifice very much greater than the policy of stabilisation demands. Of overwhelming importance is the question of unemployment. We are unhesitatingly of the opinion that without a drop in the *Real* as distinguished from the nominal wage level, the unemployment menace cannot be met; and without reasonable stability of the price level, its reduction must be postponed for many years.[1]

Whether we take this as a basis for "the middle course" or the economic policy embodied in the May 1931 Report of the Copland Committee, or again the policy suggested

---

[1] On reflection an important flaw in the argument of this memorandum is apparent. No consideration was given to the problem of investment, the volume of which was likely to be reduced by the depression. This problem is discussed in Lecture VIII.

by the Wallace Bruce Committee of April 1932, or finally the three manifestos issued by the economists, we find with varying emphasis the same economic philosophy. The restoration of economic equilibrium is largely a matter of lifting the burden of loss from export producers. The attainment of budget equilibrium depends in part upon economies and in part upon a restoration of money income. Action to attain economic and budgetary balance must be conditioned by such practical considerations as business confidence and social pressures. Advances are necessary along two main fronts, the direct attack on costs and the exploitation of monetary policy. In the first we have the pruning of government expenditure and the reduction in real wages and fixed charges of 10%. In the second we have currency depreciation and the expansion of central bank credit. There is a well-considered mingling of deflation and inflation aiming at limiting the loss of money income and spreading that loss as rapidly and equitably as possible. Theoretically, the original conception of the middle course as a plan of stabilisation is preferable. In practice, with continued and heavy deflation abroad, it was not possible to achieve it, but the main ideas embodied in that plan have been the guiding principle of Australian economic policy since the adoption of the Premiers' Plan in June 1931. How that policy has developed and what are its effects to date will be discussed in Lectures V–VIII. We must pause here and examine in the next lecture the interesting machinery of national economic administration, to which I referred in the first lecture. It was this machinery that imparted a high degree of flexibility to the Australian economic structure.

IV

THE FLEXIBILITY OF INSTITUTIONS

I. *Elements of Pre-Depression Rigidity*

BEFORE the depression the Australian economy was regarded both at home and abroad as one of the most rigid in the world. The conception of the standard of living was firmly rooted in the public mind. We have seen that an attempt to modify the arbitration system in 1929 was interpreted as an attack on the standard of living. In no uncertain manner did the electorate reject the proposal. Later, in November 1930, when the Melbourne Agreement formed the main issue at the New South Wales State elections, the opponents of the Agreement secured a very large majority. With an elaborate system of wage regulation, a high tariff, a rooted objection to reducing government expenditure and a firm belief in parity with sterling as the guiding principle in monetary policy, there seemed little chance of bending the Australian economy to the new conditions imposed by the depression.

Each of the powerful interests likely to control policy in one of these vital matters was firmly convinced that any change would be disastrous, not only to the special interests concerned but also to the nation as a whole. Thus the manufacturing industries could not conceive that any lowering of the tariff would be of benefit to the nation, and certainly it offered little direct assistance to them. They desired and secured a rise in the tariff when the competition of imports at lower prices became vigorous. The banks and financial institutions, especially those directed from London, held fast to the idea of parity with sterling. Wage earners were naturally opposed to a reduction in the standard of living, and they urged that deflationary action of this kind would only intensify the depression. There was great political opposition to reductions in government expenditure. This opposition was stimulated by many who had formerly been engaged in industries dependent upon loan expenditure.

In these circumstances, the natural resistances of all economic systems to rapid adjustments were greatly strengthened in Australia. Another force operating to promote rigidity was the somewhat cumbersome political system. The six State Governments had wide powers, and resented the intrusion of the Commonwealth into spheres of activity that had formerly been their own preserve. Considerable overlapping of expenditure between the Commonwealth and the States had developed in the period of prosperity when the Commonwealth had surpluses to spend. There had been much discussion and negotiation before the depression on this problem of overlapping, but the centripetal tendencies of Commonwealth administration were not to be easily reconciled with State rights. With this fundamental cleavage between the Commonwealth and the States, with, in addition, acute differences among the States themselves, the task of organising a common attack upon the budgetary problem and economic adjustment generally was formidable. Even within Australia there were grave doubts as to the ability of the country to modify its political and economic system for the purpose of making the necessary adjustments. This fear undoubtedly influenced the trend of economic thought, and the nature of the plan as ultimately developed from the arguments of the economists on the one hand, and the pressure of political and business opinion on the other.

II. *Causes of Flexibility in the Crisis*

We have seen that the loss of income in the crisis was one-third at its lowest point. We have seen also that the disorganisation caused by this heavy loss affected all branches of economic activity. The adjustments necessary to spread the loss rapidly, to check the fall of income and to lay the foundations for economic recovery were drastic. They were for the most part taken within two years of the onset of the depression. Their adoption involved the surrender of cherished ideas by all responsible groups and the modification of the working of some important institutions that formed what I propose to call the machinery of national economic administration. We have to enquire how it was possible to give to the Australian economy a powerful ingredient of flexibility. There are two main lines of explanation. First, the peculiar nature of the institutions of control as developed in the era of prosperity made them, and the whole structure, much more flexible than was thought possible in 1930. Second, the public discussions on the national income and the loss suffered in the depression convinced the average man that some measure of adjustment was inevitable. No doubt the post-war inflation experiences in Europe had their influence, and were probably responsible for the unfavourable reception accorded Mr Theodore when he submitted his inflationary proposals to popular audiences in April 1931. Be that as it may, there was a general feeling of relief when the plan enunciated by the Committee of Under-Treasurers and Economists in May 1931 was made public. It was a plan that contained ideas already familiar in public discussion, and it carried conviction with the general public. We shall deal with this in Lecture VI, and must defer further discussion of it.

Turning to the first, and perhaps the most important

explanation of the surprising flexibility of the Australian economic structure, we have to consider three main institutions, namely, the Loan Council, the Commonwealth Bank and the Arbitration Court.[1] We deal with the Loan Council first.

III. *The Financial Agreement and the Loan Council*

An adequate treatment of the steps leading to the formation of the Loan Council and of its subsequent influence upon Australian politics is a subject for the constitutional lawyer and not for the economist. It is necessary for our purpose, however, to consider briefly the constitutional problem involved, and I shall attempt to sketch it for you.[2] A financial agreement between the Commonwealth and the States was reached on December 12th, 1927. The main features of this agreement for our present purpose may be stated as follows:

(1) The Commonwealth was to take over the whole of the public debts of the States.

(2) The Commonwealth was to apply £7,584,912 annually from its revenues towards payment of the interest charges, and the States to contribute the balance of interest payments on their debts.

---

[1] The correct title of the Court is the Commonwealth Court of Conciliation and Arbitration. Though I shall speak of it as the Arbitration Court, I do not mean to imply that the element of conciliation was not important.

[2] The problem is discussed in the Report of the Royal Commission on the Constitution, 1928; in Sir Edward Mitchell's *What Every Australian Ought to Know*; in an article by Norman Cowper in *The Economic Record* for December 1932; in a paper, "The First Financial Agreement" by H. S. Nicholas, read before a conference of the Australian Institute of Politics in January 1933; in Portus (Editor), *Studies in the Australian Constitution* (Angus and Robertson); and in an article by O. de R. Foenander on "The Struggle between the Commonwealth of Australia and the State of New South Wales", *Archiv für Öffentliches Recht*, 1933. In articles in *The Economic Journal* of September 1924 and December 1927, I discussed the history of the financial relations of the States and the Commonwealth and the agreement of 1927 that led to an important alteration in the constitution, and to the establishment of the Loan Council with its present powers for the control of loan expenditure. The financial agreement of 1927 is reprinted in *The Commonwealth Year Book*, No. 25, of 1932.

(3) A sinking fund of 2*s*. 6*d*. % per annum by the Commonwealth and 5*s*. % per annum by the States was to be established for the extinction of the State debts taken over by the Commonwealth.

(4) On all new debt the sinking fund was to be 10*s*. % per annum, of which the Commonwealth would contribute 5*s*. and the States 5*s*.

(5) The management of the debt and future borrowing on behalf of the Commonwealth and the States was to be vested in an Australian Loan Council, consisting of a representative of the Commonwealth and a representative of each State.

The agreement required an amendment of the constitution and subsequent legislation by the seven parliaments concerned. The constitutional amendment was to Clause 105 of the Commonwealth Constitution. This clause had originally given the Commonwealth the right to "take over from the States their public debts existing at the establishment of the Commonwealth". In 1910 a constitutional amendment, the only important one hitherto approved by referendum, deleted from Clause 105 the words: "existing at the establishment of the Commonwealth". Under this amendment, the Commonwealth was able to take over the whole of the debts at any time by agreement with the States. The new amendment was intended to give parliament power to make laws with respect to the State debts "for carrying out or giving effect to any agreement made or to be made between the Commonwealth and the States". The amendment was carried in 1928, and in 1929 the Commonwealth Parliament passed "The Financial Agreement Validation Act 1929". This legislation, together with State Validation Acts, made the financial agreement of 1927 binding on the six States and the Commonwealth as parties to it. The agreement can, however, be varied or rescinded by common action, but, as subsequent events showed, it is legally binding on each party unless all agree to a modification.

Its effect upon the financial relations of the States and the Commonwealth are of much interest to the student of public finance in a federation; but I must pass over this problem. We are concerned here only with the effects of the financial agreement upon financial administration. Let us consider the powers of the Loan Council as finally established. The representatives of the States on the Council have one vote each, but the Commonwealth has two and, if necessary, the casting vote in addition. No doubt the high voting power of the Commonwealth is a recognition of the increased responsibility it assumed in regard to the State debts, a responsibility which was soon to be rather heavier than was at first anticipated. The Loan Council is authorised to regulate public borrowing. The amount and the terms of loans to be raised must be approved by the Loan Council. After 1930, as indicated below, loans for financing deficits came under the control of the Council. In addition, the Council must settle the terms for the conversion, renewal or redemption of existing loans.[1]

We see here a deliberate attempt on the part of the Commonwealth and State Governments to set up a statutory body with the right to limit and control the borrowing powers of the seven Governments. This made a radical change in the machinery of government in Australia. In the words of Mr H. S. Nicholas: "The Loan Council is an executive and representative body controlling the development of each State, yet not directly responsible to any Parliament or any Electorate". As the depression developed, the Loan Council, with its wide powers to control

[1] The only public loans excluded from the jurisdiction of the Loan Council are loans for defence purposes by the Commonwealth, loans for public statutory bodies such as the Melbourne Metropolitan Board of Works, and loans for temporary purposes, where the funds are obtained on current account and no security is given.

borrowing, quickly became the central directing authority of financial policy. As budget deficits increased, the control of borrowing for meeting deficits passed into the hands of the Council. Temporary bank accommodation no longer sufficed for meeting current expenditure, and the power of the Council to control borrowing for deficits gave it also the power of fixing the deficits. The treasury bill was devised as the method of deficit finance, and subsequently also as the method of financing a limited programme of loan expenditure.[1] The amount, the duration and rate of interest on the bills were fixed by the Council in agreement with the Commonwealth Bank, which issued the bills. The Bank accepted the responsibility of rediscounting the bills, and they became securities open to investment by the trading banks. Up to the present the market for the bills is limited to the banks. This again is a matter that falls under the control of the Loan Council, in consultation with the Commonwealth Bank. When the Chairman of the Commonwealth Bank announced on behalf of the Bank the decision not to extend further credits to the governments pending the development of a more satisfactory budget plan, he wrote to the Commonwealth Treasurer in the capacity of the latter as Chairman of the Loan Council and not as Treasurer of the Commonwealth. I quote from the letter of the Chairman of the Bank of April 2nd, 1931. "It

---

[1] In his letter to the Chairman of the Loan Council of December 13th, 1930, Sir Robert Gibson, as Chairman of a Bankers' Conference, wrote as follows: "The position has become so difficult that the banks have been forced to adopt a definite attitude and lay down principles that all advances made to governments should be approved by the Loan Council and arranged for by that body as the central authority. So as to provide the necessary machinery for carrying this into effect, the banks propose that financial assistance to be given to any government shall be covered by treasury bills issued under the authority of the Loan Council, to which body the banks will look for the discharge of the obligations created by the issue of these bills. This brings the position, therefore, to a definite point, and the banks can in future only consider the total amount of assistance which can be made available to all the governments in the light of the ability of the banks for the time being to make available such total assistance".

now becomes the unpleasant duty of the board to advise the Loan Council that a point is being reached beyond which it would be impossible for the Bank to provide further assistance for the Governments in the future."[1] This decision was resented by the Commonwealth Treasurer (here I might say in his capacity as Treasurer of the Commonwealth and not as Chairman of the Loan Council) as being "an attempt on the part of the Bank to arrogate to itself a supremacy over the Government in the determination of the financial policy of the Commonwealth". It was, of course, nothing of the kind, but merely a correct method of conveying to the governments of Australia a decision by the Board of the Bank. The limits set by the Board were £25 m. treasury bills or overdrafts within Australia, and the existing bills and debentures advanced in London amounting to £25,125,000. It was a matter for the Loan Council to decide whether the limit was reasonable, and the Commonwealth Treasurer knew that the Loan Council on the whole agreed with the Chairman of the Bank.

We thus see to what extent the Loan Council could exercise a determining influence upon financial policy in Australia. The Council could even refuse to sanction continued borrowing for deficits by the Commonwealth Parliament, and it certainly set limits to the deficits of the States. The exercise of this power was within the terms of the Agreement, though it was not perhaps realised when the Agreement was formulated. To quote again from Mr Nicholas: "Other instances might be given of the control of the Council or of the banks of a State policy, instances in which States have been refused a portion of their Treasury Bill requirements but have been given a lesser amount on condition that they have imposed new taxes or new economies. The stability of Australian finance may

---

[1] This letter, together with the reply of the Chairman of the Loan Council, are published in Shann and Copland, *The Battle of the Plans*, pp. 44–56.

have benefited by this exercise of power, and it is clearly within the terms of the agreement, but I doubt whether anyone can say that it was within the contemplation of the signatories to the agreement".

IV. *The Loan Council and State Powers*

The Loan Council could thus become a channel through which the Commonwealth Bank could influence financial policy. The Council could itself impose a common budgetary policy upon Australian Governments. It thus became the effective instrument through which economies and new forms of revenue were forced upon even unwilling governments. But it had positive and still more constructive activities. The use of the treasury bill sanctioned by the Council and issued by the Commonwealth Bank became a means by which rapid expansion of central bank credit was possible without creating fears of inflation. According to the Premiers' Plan, which was itself the outcome of pressure from a majority in the Loan Council, deficits were to be controlled and treasury bills for financing them were to be issued by the Commonwealth Bank under authority from the Loan Council. This gave what appeared to the public a proper sanction to the expansion of central bank credit for financing deficits. The same is true of the treasury bills issued for the purpose of maintaining a limited programme of loan works. Without the Loan Council it would have been impossible to embark upon this experiment in controlled inflation.

In the Financial Agreement the Commonwealth became responsible for the payment of interest upon the State debts. Part 3 of the Agreement provided for the taking over of the debts by the Commonwealth which "will in respect of the debts so taken over assume as between the Commonwealth and the States the liabilities of the States to bondholders". The complete liability of the Commonwealth for the State debts was affirmed in the "Financial Agreement (Commonwealth Liability) Act 1932". Having accepted this responsibility, the Commonwealth desired to ensure that all States would meet their obligations under the Agreement. When New South Wales first defaulted on its overseas interest in 1931, proceedings against that State were initiated in the High Court by the Commonwealth. When the Premiers' Plan was formulated, New South Wales agreed to resume interest payments, but defaulted again in January 1932. On this occasion, the Commonwealth took much more drastic action against the State. In "The Financial Agreements Enforcement Act" and in "The Financial Agreements (Commonwealth Liability) Act", the Commonwealth obtained power to recover from a State by a suit in the High Court any monies payable by the State under the Financial Agreement and for which the Commonwealth had become liable. Machinery was also provided by this legislation for ensuring that the Commonwealth could obtain from the State a refund of monies that it had disbursed to creditors of the State in question. There followed a very interesting struggle between New South Wales and the Commonwealth, with full legal honours to the Commonwealth. So powerful had the Commonwealth become under the Financial Agreement and the new legislation, that it was able to acquire rights to practically the whole tax revenue of the New South Wales Government, provided the funds so acquired were necessary to meet interest payments made on behalf of the State. For the time being the State of New South Wales was gradually coming under the direct control of the Commonwealth, and the State Government was experiencing increasing difficulties in maintaining the ordinary machinery of government. The struggle ended with the complete victory of the Commonwealth and with the principle established that a State which fails to meet its interest obligations may have its independence destroyed. Though the other State Governments were strongly opposed to the policy pursued by the New South Wales Government of the day, two of the States, Victoria and Tasmania, opposed the Commonwealth on the constitutional issue in the High Court, on the ground that the powers sought by the Commonwealth were contrary to the spirit of the constitution, which was intended to safeguard the independence of the States.

We see therefore that the Financial Agreement enabled the Commonwealth to make agreements which parliament could not alter during a specified period, but an agreement has the great merit that changing economic and social conditions may be recognised rapidly by an alteration of the terms of the Agreement if the seven parties to it are unanimous. The Financial Agreement is in effect part of the constitution, but is more flexible than the constitution. We also observe that the power of the Commonwealth to control the social and economic policy of a State has been greatly enhanced by the Agreement. If the States are agreed among themselves, they can always secure a majority in the Loan Council, but the Commonwealth has much more influence than any State and can normally obtain a veto on State proposals to which it is opposed. On the other hand, the Loan Council may be instrumental, as it was in 1931, in forcing the Commonwealth to participate in a policy to which it was originally opposed.

V. *Development of the Commonwealth Bank*

Working in close co-operation with the Loan Council, the Commonwealth Bank has steadily acquired virtually all the functions of a central bank. The legislation passed in October 1924 was designed to promote the development of the Bank as a central reserve bank. I have given an account of this legislation and of the subsequent developments in bank policy in *Credit and Currency Control*, Chap. II.

It will be sufficient to recall here that the 1924 legislation made provision for the appointment of a board of directors, for the control of the note issue by the Bank, for the increase in the capital of the Bank, and for the settlement of clearing transactions through the Bank. The new board did not embark upon an active trading policy in competition with the private banks, though in 1925 they established a rural credits department for providing short-term credit on primary products awaiting sale. This department has been very successful and does not in any way seem to conflict with the principle that a central bank should keep its assets highly liquid. The savings bank was separated from the other branches of the Bank in 1927, although still under the ultimate control of the board. The Bank thus had on the eve of the crisis an issue and banking department, on the plan of the Bank of England, a savings bank and a rural credits department. The legal reserve against the note issue was 25% in gold, and the 1924 Act allowed notes to be issued against Australian or British Government securities and approved short-term bills.

To an increasing extent between 1925 and 1929 the Bank assumed the normal operations undertaken by a central bank for a government. When the crisis commenced to disorganise the balance of payments, the Bank naturally accepted some responsibility for maintaining a liquid position in London. In October 1929 the Chairman wrote to the Commonwealth Treasurer, drawing his attention to the difficulties of maintaining overseas reserves while meeting external obligations. He urged the Government to pass legislation giving the Bank immediate control of all the gold in Australia. At that time the trading banks held gold to the amount of £24 m. The legislation was passed in November, and gold reserves became centralised under the control of the Bank. The reserves, however, were required for external payments, and the amount taken from the trading banks was soon used up in this way. Whatever the special effects of this action were at the moment, the new legislation marked another step in the progress of the Bank towards its goal as a central bank.

Two other important amendments were made to the Bank Act during the crisis. In June 1931, after the adoption of the Premiers' Plan, the reserve requirements against the note issue were reduced from 25% to 15%, with the provision that the 25% reserve should be restored in steps by July 1st, 1935. The amendment was required to enable the Government to use a portion of the Bank's gold reserve for meeting maturing short-term obligations in London. It is important to add that the Government did not acquire rights to this gold without the consent of the Bank board. The second amendment was made in May 1932. The new legislation again dealt with the reserve against the note issue. It was provided that the legal reserve could be held in "English sterling" or in gold. English sterling was defined to include bills at the Bank of England, bills of exchange that will mature in not more than three months payable in United Kingdom currency, and treasury bills of the United Kingdom that will mature in not more than three months. The fiction of convertibility of the note into gold was deleted and nothing substituted for it. The Bank was empowered to transfer its gold reserves to sterling reserves, and any profit accruing on this transaction was to be transferred to a special reserve and to be available "from time to time as the board determines for the purpose of stabilising exchange or for the purposes of the Note Issue Department". This legislation is very important in that it implies that sterling and not gold is the legal basis of Australian currency, but it does not fix any special rate at which the Australian note shall be convertible into sterling. Indeed it does not specify that the Australian note shall be convertible into anything at all. The Bank board has thus very wide powers of control over the currency, and is probably more independent in this respect than the Bank of England. In England the Gold Standard (Amendment) Act 1931 relieved the Bank of England for two years from September 18th, 1931, of the obligation to sell gold bullion for notes. In the case of Australia there is nothing in the present legislation requiring the Bank to pay out gold or sterling or any other currency in exchange for notes. The Bank is free to manage the currency according to its discretion for the time being, though the Government may at any time amend the Act, limiting the discretion of the Bank.

It is not only in respect of its freedom of action in determining the relationship of Australian currency to external currency that the Commonwealth Bank has acquired exceptional powers. It is not bound by any conditions limiting its right to make advances to governments, to banks or to individuals. There was, for example, nothing to prevent the Bank from extending freely its unsecured overdrafts to governments. The Bank wisely refused to pursue such a course, but it proceeded to make credit available to governments on the security of short-term bills. These might be purchased by the trading banks, but were discountable at the Commonwealth Bank. This is not usual in the charters of central banks established since the war in countries with a dependent monetary and financial economy.[1] It was within the discretion of the

---

[1] After surveying the limited powers of modern central banks to grant credits to Governments, Kisch and Elkin, *Central Banks*, p. 35, remark that "it is of first-rate importance that it should be made as difficult as possible for the Governments to resort to the expedient of borrowing from the Bank, a practice which, if continued, can only lead to a repetition of past disasters. At least, such clauses indicate a standard of wise finance, the formal recognition of which is likely to have some influence, and the provisions carry the safeguard that if there is a question of increasing the amount of the State credits, the matter must be brought before the Legislature and cannot legally be effected by mere pressure on the Bank". In Australia there was no need to bring before Parliament the question of increasing credits to the Government. Australian experience of a controlled expansion of credit throws doubt upon the necessity or wisdom of restricting the freedom of action of a central bank.

board to make credit available to governments in this way. The Bank was under no obligation to meet all the demands of government. Though it made advances available freely at first, it ultimately asserted its independence and was in large part responsible for checking the drift in public finance. Its policy, however, as we shall see later, was constructive, especially as regards exchange management and the expansion of central bank credit. Its freedom of action enabled it in December 1931 to undertake the purchase and sale of London funds at rates fixed by the Bank. Thus in all matters of currency management the Bank assumed complete control, subject to one limitation only. This was its legal obligation to hold a reserve against the note issue. As already stated on p. 85 this obligation was relaxed during the depression. From May 1932 the reserve became English sterling without alteration in the percentage required. The Bank was empowered to use any profits on the transfer of gold to sterling for the purposes already mentioned.[1] These wide powers might have been used unwisely if the Bank had come under the domination of political leaders determined on an extreme policy of either deflation or inflation. Fortunately the Bank pursued an independent middle course between these two extremes and was on the whole able to withstand pressure from business or banking interests.

VI. *The Arbitration Court*

The third institution that calls for comment is the Arbitration Court. The wage-fixing machinery of Australia is so well known to students of labour problems that I need not enter into a detailed discussion of it here.[2] At the com-

---

[1] See p. 85.
[2] See in particular the standard work on the subject, George Anderson, *Wage Fixation in Australia* (Melbourne University Press), and also his articles in *The Economic Record* for November 1928 and November 1930.

mencement of the crisis the position was briefly as follows: The Commonwealth Court was the main wage-fixing authority. The legal definition of a "dispute" had overcome to a large extent the limitation imposed upon the Court by the Constitution, namely that the Commonwealth had powers to make laws for "conciliation and arbitration for the prevention and settlement of industrial disputes extending beyond the limits of any one State". By a decision of the High Court in 1926 Commonwealth awards in any industry took precedence over State awards. There were State courts in New South Wales, Queensland, South Australia and Western Australia, and wages boards in Victoria and Tasmania. The latter tended to follow the wage standards fixed by the Commonwealth Court. This was true also of the State courts, with the possible exception of the New South Wales court, where State legislation had defined more rigidly the living wage and had established a scheme for child endowment.[1]

The Commonwealth Court was working on a wage standard determined by the so-called "Harvester Case" of 1907, which fixed 7s. a day as the living wage. To this had been added in 1922 the "Powers' 3s." a week, an addition to the basic wage, usually ascribed to the desire of the Court to compensate wage earners for losses of real wages incurred during the wartime inflation. This standard wage was adjusted quarterly according to movements in a cost of living index covering food, groceries, fuel and light, and house rent. The Court was, however, influenced, as were the State courts, by general economic conditions and the special economic conditions of each industry. It could not legally establish a common rule; hence every case had to be heard on its merits and every employer had to be cited.

---

[1] In Queensland the State court had given much attention to local economic conditions, and wages were high in industries controlled by the court. But Queensland is a non-industrial State.

I do not propose to discuss the disputed question as to whether the Court raised wages above the economic level, though I may recall what I said on this point in Lecture I.[1] We may note, however, that the Court did bring into the scheme of wage fixation large numbers of workers that were formerly not organised and received wages below the level fixed by the Court. Though unable to establish a common rule in law, the operation of the Court had in fact extended to casual labour and to "the black-coated brigade" a wage rate not lower than the Harvester standard. In 1929 and 1930 some of the States, especially New South Wales and Queensland, passed legislation suspending State awards in rural industries. The powers of the Commonwealth Court had not been checked, except in respect of the condition that the basic wage in an industry could be altered only by a bench of three judges. Further, the Court was instructed by Parliament to consider economic conditions in determining its awards. But the Court was independent of Parliament, subject, of course, to changes in the law as determined by Parliament.[2] This fact was amply demonstrated by the attitude of the Court during the hearing of the basic wage case from October 1930 to January 1931. It will be remembered that the Government of the day had been elected on a pledge to preserve the Court. This was interpreted by the electorate as a pledge to preserve the standard of living. Despite important amendments to the Arbitration Act, the Government was powerless to prevent the Court from ordering a reduction in wages, if economic conditions appeared to

[1] See p. 18.
[2] From time to time the judges of the Court have referred to this fact during the hearing of a case. In the award on January 22nd, 1930, on the important basic wage case, the Court, referring to the distribution of profits by companies, remarked: "The basis of past distribution has been under an established economic system controlled by the legislature, and, as we have often pointed out, this Court is not the legislature, but functions in an economic system which the legislature alone can alter".

necessitate such a reduction. The Government did in fact intervene in the case, and was represented by counsel. This was the limit to its authority, and the Court, after hearing evidence that covered the whole economic position of the country, decided to reduce the basic wage by 10% in addition to the normal adjustments of the wage to quarterly decreases in the cost of living. The award of the Court was a survey of the general economic situation at the end of 1930, and it is of more than passing interest to note that the first pronouncement on the crisis from a responsible authority was this award of the Arbitration Court. As indicated in the first lecture, this pronouncement and the reduction in the real wage of 10% was accepted as the basis of direct adjustments in all costs made later in the Premiers' Plan. The Court, with its independent position and its known sympathy in the past with the demands for as high a standard of living as the country could afford, was well fitted to call attention to the economic position and to the need for general adjustment. In its award, the Court referred to budgetary and currency policy, though, of course, its authority for action was confined to the determination of wage rates. The decision in the basic wage case was made in respect of certain railway applications, but was quickly extended to practically all other industries under the authority of the Court. All awards were varied in accordance with this decision, and the net effect was to impart to the wage structure of Australia a flexibility that would not have been possible without the authority of the Court.

It will be necessary in Lecture VI to deal with the attitude of the other wage-fixing authorities, and in particular with the attempt in New South Wales to maintain rigidity in the wage structure. Given the general acceptance of the policy on banking, on budgets and on costs of industry that developed in 1931, this attempt to maintain rigid wage rates was bound to fail, and fail it did. The survey now completed of the three main institutions of national economic administration establishes quite clearly that this machinery was, on the political philosophy of the moment, outside the control of the legislature. The Loan Council in particular was in an impregnable position. Had not the Commonwealth Senate opposed governmental policy, drastic changes might have been made in the constitution of the Commonwealth Bank and in the legal position of the Arbitration Court. In the latter case, however, the Commonwealth constitution itself was a barrier to drastic change. With a willing Senate, the banking system could have been brought under the control of the Government, and this would doubtless have altered completely the policy pursued by Australia, and in fact laid down and administered by the three independent bodies I have been discussing. Their independence and their capacity to pursue a courageous course imparted the element of flexibility to the whole economic structure that was necessary for the policy of economic adjustment that followed.

V

THE BALANCE OF PAYMENTS AND EXCHANGE CONTROL

I. *Disturbance and Recovery in the Balance*

I N Lecture II we noted that the first impact of the crisis on the Australian economy was a dislocation of the balance of payments. The extent to which Australian income from abroad was disturbed has been strikingly illustrated by a comparison of the balance of payments in gold currency for the year 1931/32 and the average for the years 1923–29. In the latter years, the debits were: imports £151 m. and interest and sinking fund £26 m., making a total of £177 m. The credits were: exports £147 m., loans £27 m., leaving a "deficiency" of £3 m. For 1931/32, imports at the same volume as for 1923–29 would have amounted to £83 m. and interest and sinking fund to £30 m. Exports at the old level would have amounted to £48 m. As long-term borrowing had ceased the "deficiency" was £65 m.[1] This comparison, though crude, demonstrates the nature of the problem confronting Australia in adjusting her balance of payments to the new conditions imposed by the crisis.

Thanks to the investigations of Dr Roland Wilson we have a more detailed estimate of the balance of payments for the period 1928/29 to 1931/32.[2]

I propose to quote Dr Wilson's Summary Tables (see p. 93).

The measure of recovery in 1931/32 is a striking achievement in face of adverse conditions as to export prices and

---

[1] Davidson, *Australia's Share in International Recovery* (the Joseph Fisher Lecture in Commerce at the University of Adelaide, July 1932).

[2] Wilson, *The Australian Balance of Payments* (Supplement to *The Economic Record*, October 1932).

overseas credits operating at the time. The current account favourable balance of £15 m. was attained despite the fact that export prices in sterling were over 50 % below the pre-crisis level. Perhaps, however, the most striking feature of the table is the aggregate unfavourable balance on current account of £82·4 m. for the years 1928/29 and 1929/30. This unfavourable balance, be it noted, was incurred despite

Current movements of goods, services and gold	1928/29	1929/30	1930/31	1931/32
Inward or credit movements (exports):	£,000 stg.	£,000 stg.	£,000 stg.	£,000 stg.
I. Merchandise	141,004	100,878	79,485	80,395
II. Interest and dividends	2,437	2,553	2,350	2,499
III. Other services	13,293	13,372	10,792	7,859
IV. Gold coin and bullion	1,116	24,999	10,120	5,901
Total credits	157,850	141,802	102,747	96,654
Outward or debit movements (imports):				
I. Merchandise	149,389	138,535	64,119	47,362
II. Interest and dividends	37,414	38,451	36,279	30,137
III. Other services	9,391	8,234	5,123	3,528
IV. Gold coin and bullion	348	294	374	631
Total debits	196,542	185,514	105,895	81,658
Excess of debits (−) or credits (+)	−38,692	−43,712	−3,148	+14,996

specie exports in 1929/30 of £25 m. of which £22 m. was taken from gold reserves. Had this export of specie been sufficient to balance the accounts the effort to maintain exchange at or near par up to the end of 1930 would not have been surprising, but when the use of gold reserves on a liberal scale was accompanied by a heavy deficit on current account in the balance of payments, the official exchange policy pursued up to the end of 1930 cannot be justified. In their report of January 24th, 1930, the Directors of the Commonwealth Bank stated the policy of the Bank with regard to exchange in the following terms:

So far as the Bank board is concerned, it could not possibly desire to advise any action which would savour of Australia departing from the gold standard; on the other hand, it is absolutely necessary on behalf of the board of the Bank, that the position must be controlled and the available gold used in such manner as will avoid more serious embarrassment, and that it should be used in the best interests of Australia by one authority which is in possession of the knowledge necessary to direct and control its use to these ends.[1]

The policy of attempting to maintain the gold standard, or at least of pegging the exchange rate close to parity, was pursued by most of the banking authorities and by the Government during the whole of 1930.[2] It was abandoned early in 1931 when fears of currency inflation stimulated a flight of capital and reinforced the influence of a fall in export prices in depleting our London reserves. Investigations into the balances of banking funds held in London before the depression showed that in the favourable years

[1] Quoted in Shann and Copland, *The Crisis in Australian Finance* (p. 6). It will be remembered that the Board in October 1929 had advised the Commonwealth Treasurer to pass legislation empowering the Bank to take over on behalf of the Government the gold reserves of the Commonwealth. In fact Australia abandoned the gold standard when this legislation was passed.

[2] This policy was supported by governments in the belief that a low exchange rate (relatively small depreciation on sterling) would ease the task of meeting external interest obligations. I deal with this problem later in this lecture. Here it is necessary to note that this belief, together with the desire of the banks also to keep the rate low, led in September 1930 to the formation of the voluntary exchange pool referred to in Lecture III above (p. 52). This pool could have been successful only as "a temporary expedient pending a general deflation of costs in Australia", as I pointed out at the time (*Credit and Currency Control*, p. 10). But the magnitude of the deflation was too great for the success of a policy that attempted to maintain heavy over-valuation of the currency. Later, when the rate of exchange was raised and the programme of economic adjustment expedited, the pool became unnecessary. It remained as a convenient means through which the Commonwealth Bank purchased, on behalf of the Government, the necessary exchange to meet external commitments as they fell due. Even for this purpose the pool is not necessary. Restrictions on exchange were not imposed except by "rationing" methods of the banks which were not necessary when the effort to over-value the currency was abandoned.

from 1922 to 1929 it was customary for the banks as a whole to hold some £45 m. in sterling or other assets abroad. In addition there was approximately £50 m. in gold in the reserves of the Commonwealth and private banks, making a total of £95 m. On July 1st, 1930, the estimated banking reserves abroad had fallen to £16·6 m., and the total gold reserves in Australia were about £17 m., making a total of about £34 m. On July 1st, 1931, a further slight fall had taken place. The important fact to note here is that gold reserves and banking assets abroad had been reduced by about £65 m. in the period of two years when the balance of payments was heavily unfavourable to Australia, and the exchange rate was maintained at a point that over-valued the Australian currency.

Before dealing with the effects of currency depreciation upon the Australian economy, we may pause to enquire why the unhappy position of the balance of payments in 1929/30 was so rapidly transformed into a favourable situation in 1931/32. Using the figures contained in the above Summary Table, and bearing in mind that they are expressed in sterling values, we may note the following developments favourable to Australia's external balance of accounts.

(*a*) The fall of over 50 % in the sterling prices of export was to some extent counterbalanced by the expansion of over 25 % in the volume of Australian exports.

(*b*) The concession of £5·5 m. on account of War Debt payments to Great Britain and the reduction in dividends gave relief to the extent of £7 m.

(*c*) But the greatest source of adjustment was the very low level to which imports fell in 1931/32. They were on the average less than £4 m. per month compared with £12·5 m. before the depression. To some extent this would be accounted for by a fall in the price level of imports, but the major influence was a heavy reduction in the volume of imports. It was generally recognised at the time, that imports at £4 m. sterling were inadequate to maintain industry and to meet the normal demands of consumption at the prevailing standard of living.[1]

II. *Parity with Gold versus Parity with Sterling*

We now proceed to consider the more important effects on the Australian economy of the depreciation of the currency. To some extent this problem has been discussed in Lecture II, but I propose here to state concisely the general case for and against a depreciation of the currency in a country with a large volume of export production of which the supply is inelastic. The discussion has special reference to the arguments used in recent Australian controversy on the exchange problem. It will be assumed, however, that the depreciation of the currency is one element of a general policy involving

(*a*) direct reductions in costs, and

(*b*) expansion of credit, especially for public works and budget deficits.

Moreover, in the case of Australia, which entered the depression so much earlier than other countries, we must assume that the depreciation of the currency was not part of a general world currency depreciation, though this developed later. It is reasonable to suppose, in these circumstances, that the national income would on the whole retain its previous relationship to the value of exports. I shall therefore assume that the national income would tend to settle at from 4 to 4½ times the value of ex-

---

[1] The actual decline in the volume of imports was at least 50%. On the assumption that sterling prices of imports fell by one-third, imports of £150 m. would have cost only £100 m. At the lower price level in 1931/32 they were less than £50 m. The low level of imports was, of course, an indication of the serious decline in internal spending power, and confirmed the principle that imports fluctuate with the level of prosperity, despite tariffs.

ports.[1] This was the ratio in the pre-depression period, and it would not be changed much in a short period of three years.

We take the year 1931/32 as the basis for our statement of the problem. In that year there had been an expansion of export production of over 25 % compared with the three years before the depression. I will assume that this expansion would have taken place had Australia remained on the gold standard, an assumption which unduly favours the case for maintaining the gold standard. The sterling value of exports of 1931/32 was, approximately, £80 m. On the assumption we have made we get the following results for the national income at different rates of exchange:

	Export prices, June 1932 (1928 = 100)	Estimated value of exports, 1931/32	Estimated national income
		£ m.	£ m.
At parity with gold	31·5	60	260
At parity with sterling	42	80	350
At 25 % above parity with sterling	52·5	100	430

(N.B. The values given are expressed in terms of the currency that would operate in Australia on the several assumptions made.)

Despite the depreciation of sterling by about 30 % at the time no one suggested in July 1932 that Australia should return to parity with gold, and appreciate her currency in

---

[1] Given the expansion of credit to finance deficits and loan expenditure, a reduction in sterling prices temporarily on account of currency depreciation would be offset by the income derived from investment. But Australian exports are in the main inelastic in supply. Though capable of expansion under favourable seasonal conditions and in some cases by special efforts for a year or two, supply does not respond to rapid price changes. The depreciation of the currency by giving exporters a better return in Australian currency reduced losses in export production. Thus it helped to prevent a contraction of production. But on the whole the effects of a depreciation of currency on export production and world prices are very different in Australia from what they are in an industrial country like Great Britain, where the supply of export products is highly elastic.

terms of sterling. There is general agreement that parity of exchange with a depreciated sterling has economic advantages over parity with gold at the old gold content of the Australian pound. Why should this view prevail while it is argued, in some quarters, that parity with sterling is to be preferred to a depreciation of the currency in terms of sterling? We cannot assume that because parity with sterling is to be preferred to parity with gold, a depreciation in terms of sterling ought logically to be preferred to parity with sterling. An argument of this nature would set no limits to the depreciation of the currency. We must, however, investigate whether the arguments in favour of a depreciated currency in terms of gold, though at parity with sterling, are not logically applicable to a currency depreciated in terms of sterling.

The main argument in favour of parity with sterling in preference to parity with gold is, of course, the higher level of Australian export prices. Maintaining the exchange at parity with sterling does not bring any additional real income into Australia over the amount at parity with gold. But on the assumption that sterling is depreciated one-fourth in terms of the gold parity, it does support a money income in Australia at a level of $33\frac{1}{3}$% higher. By holding export prices above their level in gold it lessens the magnitude of the necessary adjustment between exporters' costs and export prices. It also lessens the extent to which all values will fall. This is important. Debts are created against securities, the value of which is determined largely by the average level of prices and the long-term profits of enterprise. If prices fall rapidly and profits are destroyed, security values also fall: but they fall in greater proportion than the fall in prices, because their value is dependent upon the profit margin. This is quickly destroyed in a period of acute deflation. Hence the value of securities upon which debts have been arranged falls rapidly until profits are restored by rising prices. All individuals and all institutions dealing in these debts must then experience difficulties in maintaining a proper balance between assets and liabilities unless they have available liquid reserves. Liabilities of financial institutions are expressed in fixed money terms, and they do not respond to a fall in prices. Hence a rapid

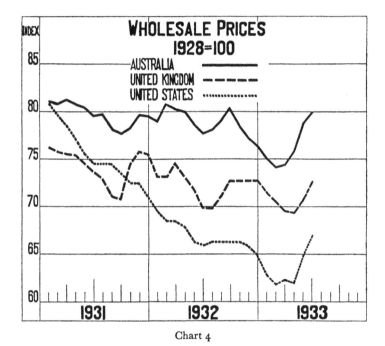

Chart 4

fall, by destroying part of the current value of assets, is likely to embarrass such institutions. The lower the new price level the greater will be the embarrassment. This is one important reason why parity with the depreciated sterling is preferred to parity with gold.

Exporters reap a benefit of higher prices in terms of the depreciated sterling, but the addition to price is paid to them by the rest of the community and not by the overseas purchaser. At parity with gold, exports would be £60 m.[1] compared with £80 m. at parity with sterling. The direct addition to exporters' income is £20 m. Who pays the additional £20 m.? We can answer this question best by considering the relative cost of imports and overseas debt charges at parity with sterling and at parity with gold. Assuming the debt charges to amount to £stg. 28 m. (we may ignore the dollar complications for the purposes of this discussion), we have £stg. 52 m. left for imports. At parity with gold the debt service would cost £21 m. in Australian (gold) currency. With exports at £60 m. imports would be £39 m. In fact there is an apparent saving of £7 m. in the external debt service and £13 m. in the cost of imports. The additional costs in terms of the depreciated sterling are thus £7 m. for debt charges and £13 m. for imports. The former is a charge on the budget and is ultimately borne by the community as a whole. The latter is a charge upon importers and is borne, in the first instance, by the purchaser of imported goods, but is spread over the rest of the community. These additional costs of the debt service and imports are thus borne by the community and paid over to the exporters, who receive a higher price in sterling for their exports. We must bear this fact in mind, because many who accept parity with sterling as a basis reject a depreciation on sterling on the ground that a bonus would be paid to the exporters by the rest of the community. This bonus would, in any case, be paid at parity with the depreciated sterling.

We may therefore conclude on this point that if the higher prices of exports in a depreciated sterling are beneficial,

---

[1] This argument ignores the transition period, during which the balance of payments is being adjusted. It assumes that exports less external obligations determine the ultimate value of imports, and that this position can be reached at the rates of exchange considered. This assumption is, of course, not strictly accurate, for the balance of payments is in part determined by the relative prices and demands for imported and home-produced goods, even though the supply of exports be highly inelastic.

still higher prices in an Australian currency depreciated in terms of sterling may be even more beneficial. We return to this problem below.

III. *Exchange and the Budget*

Consider now the effects on the budget. Interest and sinking fund on the governmental debt as a whole may be taken at approximately £55 m. at parity with sterling. The external debt charge is £28 m. We have seen that at parity with gold we would save £7 m. in this debt charge. Would this be a net saving to the budget? If we can reduce the burden of external interest by restoring parity with gold, can we hope to promote budget equilibrium through a drastic appreciation of our currency? A moment's consideration will show, however, that the saving to the budget of the appreciated currency is an illusion. The internal debt charge of £27 m. is not reduced by the appreciation of the currency, but the government revenue as a whole will be heavily reduced. We have seen that national income at parity with gold is £260 m. compared with £350 m. at parity with sterling. This is a reduction of one-fourth and we may suppose that in the long run government revenue will be reduced by approximately the same figure. But the internal interest burden will remain at its old figure, and government costs as a whole will not be easily reduced by the required one-fourth. In fact the burden of total interest payments will be increased by the appreciation of the currency, just as the burden of exporters' interest payments are increased by the same currency policy. The lower price level adds to the burden of all fixed payments. Parity with gold does not, however, reduce the real burden of the external debt. If export production is contracted it may actually increase that burden, though it reduces the nominal value of the payments. Clearly, the budget will be adversely affected by the appreciation of the currency. If this be so, might it not also be true that the budget will benefit by a depreciation of the currency in terms of sterling? Consider the 25 % rate ruling at present. This adds £7 m. to the Australian cost of external interest and makes the total interest and sinking fund about £62 m. But the national income is £430 m. in place of £350 m. The ratio of the total interest payments to national income at parity with sterling is 15·7% compared with 14·7% at a depreciation of 25 % on sterling. Moreover, total government income will tend to move with the expansion of national income to a 25 % exchange rate. Despite this higher cost in money value of the external interest payments, the budgetary problem will be easier than at parity with sterling.[1]

[1] In 1930 I drew attention to the effects of currency depreciation upon interest payments. "The burden of taxation required to meet the overseas interest payments would not be altered. The Government would have to raise in Australia sufficient taxation to buy the sterling value of the overseas interest at the current rate of exchange. The real value of the internal interest would, however, be less, and this course of action involving a slight rise in local prices would, therefore, not increase the task of financial readjustment" (*Credit and Currency Control*, p. 145). On this point and generally on the effects of currency depreciation it is worth while to recall Sir Otto Niemeyer's dictum that "rising exchange rates prejudice the whole fabric of national finance" (Address before the Premiers' Conference, August 1930, reprinted in Shann and Copland, *The Crisis of Australian Finance*, 1929–31, p. 18). No doubt this is true if we think of currency depreciation of the magnitude undertaken by some countries after the war, but circumstances were then quite different. We are here considering the economy of a primary producing country with rigid costs in its exporting industries. Moreover, the international setting is one of heavy deflation with a drastic fall in the prices of primary products. In these circumstances, a rising exchange rate so far from prejudicing the fabric of national finance, may be the chief means of preventing serious financial disorder and ensuring the payment of external interest charges. Creditor countries have shown little imagination in their attitude towards debtor and primary producing countries, who have sought relief from their burdens by depreciating their currency as part of a policy for meeting the crisis. The same attitude is to be found in companies operating in the debtor countries with headquarters in the creditor countries. Thus in the case of Australia, examples could be given of the declarations by Anglo-Australian companies as to the ill effects of currency depreciation at the very time when this depreciation was the main means of safeguarding the Australian assets of the companies concerned.

IV. *Objections to Currency Depreciation considered*

This argument supports the view urged by Australian economists in 1930 that a substantial depreciation of Australian currency in terms of sterling would be a net economic benefit to the community. Certain objections have been raised from time to time to currency depreciation. Some of these have already been answered in the argument outlined above. It will be desirable, however, to restate them.

1. There is a net cost to the community.
2. Depreciation of the currency discriminates unfairly against importers.
3. It adds to the cost of the budget.
4. It puts up the exporter's costs and destroys the benefit he receives.
5. It injures the national credit abroad.
6. It causes export prices in sterling and gold currencies to fall.

The first objection shows a complete misunderstanding of the problem. Currency depreciation on the conditions assumed and advocated by its exponents in Australia was a depreciation sufficient to assist in the restoration of economic equilibrium during the depression. Whatever may happen in a depreciation that destroys the commodity value of currencies there can be no question of net cost and disturbance to the community with the depreciation under consideration here.

With regard to No. 2 the arguments advanced by the exponents of currency depreciation as indicated in Lecture II was the importance of rapidly and equitably spreading the loss of national income. Whatever steps were taken to make the adjustment, the problem to be solved was the transfer of income from the rest of the community to export producers. In the main, deflation involved such a transfer.

The volume of exports could not be greater under deflation than under currency depreciation. This was determined by the value and volume of exports and the price level of imports. In the short period imports might be greater under deflation, but that merely exposes one of the disadvantages of deflation, viz. that the purchases of imported goods are unduly great at a time when export prices are so low. The importer ultimately passes exchange costs to the rest of the community. Whilst importing business could not but be seriously disturbed by the special circumstances of the Australian depression, the·policy of currency depreciation merely had the effect of expediting the disturbance. It may, however, have increased the volume of imports in the long run because of its encouragement to exports.

To the third objection, we have already given an adequate answer. The effect on exporters' costs raises a different problem. It is true that the depreciation of the currency will increase the costs of living, measured in Australian currency, the costs of imported goods and the wage rate. After much discussion of this problem the general conclusion is that the maximum increase in exporters' costs would be one-third of the rise in the exchange rate. It must be insisted again that costs were being reduced, especially fixed charges and wages. There is a limit to the extent of this reduction that is practicable over a short period. The higher exchange rate raises the prices of imported and exportable consumers' goods and of imported and exportable raw materials of industry. It does not immediately affect most sheltered prices, nor does it raise fixed charges. An increase of one-third in costs is to be set against an increase of three times this amount in the export prices received. If all costs could be reduced rapidly with the currency at parity with sterling the case for depreciation of currency would be much weakened. The magnitude of the problem may, however, be indicated by considering the position of the export industries. Until recently the sterling price level of exports was over 50% below the pre-depression level. Allowing for a cut of 25% in all costs this would give, on the basis of 1928 as a 100, exporters' prices at 50 and their costs at 75. The further reduction in costs required would have been of the order of 20%, bringing costs down to 60. The total reduction in costs on the 1928 level would then be at least 40%. He would be a bold man who would enter a depression with a policy designed to cut farmers' costs by 40%. The case for currency depreciation rested on the fact that it reduced the magnitude of the monetary adjustment required and added much more to exporters' prices in local currency than to exporters' costs.

As to the effect on national credit, this is plainly one of the creditors' prejudices. Experience in the crisis has dealt roughly with this prejudice, but it persists. I gave what I considered to be the economist's answer in a recent article: "The British investor does not really understand the conditions that determine your capacity to pay your interest, but he is very nervous about a high exchange rate. This, we know, is quite illogical, but you must humour your creditors as well as pay your interest. Even though a high exchange rate sustains your price level and the money value of your national income, thus lightening the real burden of your internal debt without increasing the burden of the external debt, you must forgo this measure of relief because London objects".[1]

V. *Competitive Currency Depreciation*

The last objection is, however, much more serious. It has been urged repeatedly that if all countries attempted de-

---

[1] *The Economic Journal*, September 1932, p. 379. The article dealt with the New Zealand situation but is applicable to Australia. In January 1933 New Zealand depreciated her exchange from 10 to 25% on sterling. There was no reaction on New Zealand's credit in London.

preciation of their currencies as a way out of the depression the relationship of one currency to another would be unchanged and no relief would be available. This is called *competitive currency depreciation*. The exponents of this doctrine do not usually raise objection to the much greater evils of *competitive economic deflation*, which is frequently put forward as the alternative plan of action. It is not possible to examine the full effects of the latter policy, but clearly a reduction in costs as the sole method of attack upon a depression will increase for a considerable time the difficulties of the situation. It will certainly help to lower the international price level of commodities. The alternative, so called competitive currency depreciation, is not applicable to Australian policy for the following reasons:

(*a*) Australia entered the depression earlier, at a time when the international gold standard was still firmly established. The depreciation of Australian currency could not have greatly affected the gold price level of the leading exports of Australia.

(*b*) The argument presupposes that deflation as a policy is in operation in the outside world. If this be the case any national policy will be accompanied by a fall in the international export price level, not because of the effects of the national policy, but because the forces of deflation abroad are in the ascendancy.

(*c*) A currency depreciation in Australia was not proposed as the only method of escape from the crisis, nor was it put into operation as an isolated policy. We shall see in Lecture VII that the Australian policy had a positive aspect which, if in operation in all other countries, would have checked the international deflation and prevented the monetary disasters of the past two years.

(*d*) In any case competitive currency depreciation could not have maintained the old relationships among currencies. The ratios of international exchange were upset by the conditions of the crisis, and whatever currency policy might be followed the new rates of exchange would be different from the old. In the case of Australia, the adverse terms of trade and the reduction in borrowing seriously upset the ratio of international exchange and necessitated a depreciation of Australian currency relative to sterling.

(*e*) Finally, we must not ignore the fact that heavy depreciation of currencies increases the currency value of gold and thus strengthens the hands of central banks possessing gold stocks. This would not happen under what I have called competitive economic deflation.

As far as Australia is concerned, we may test the matter by reference to the Australian export price index number, which is given in Chart 2. We observe there that from 1928 to the end of 1930 the international price of Australian exports had rapidly declined by no less than 50 %. It was in January 1931 that Australian currency was depreciated. The decline in the export price level during 1931 was less severe than for the previous two years. The percentage reduction for the years 1931 and 1932 in the gold export price level was 35 % compared with 52 % in the previous two years. This is a serious enough matter in itself, but it does not justify the conclusion that the depreciation in Australian currency in terms of gold was the cause of the fall in price. If we take the period from the departure of Great Britain from the gold standard, we find that the rate of decline in gold export prices was still less. It was the presence of international deflation that caused the decline, and not the depreciation of the Australian currency in itself.

VI. *The Limits to Currency Depreciation*

It might be assumed from this argument that there is no limit to the depreciation of the currency. Is it desirable to proceed to an unlimited rise of internal prices? I need not restate the familiar economic arguments against rapidly rising prices from a position of equilibrium, or consider their effects upon the business cycle. It is sufficient to mention these facts to give the answer to the suggestion that if a little currency depreciation is a good thing, an even greater currency depreciation will be a much better thing. The amount of currency depreciation required is, of course, determined by the equilibrium position at which the policy is aiming. The greater the practicable cuts in costs the less the degree in currency depreciation required. It is desirable, in any case, to avoid very drastic cuts in costs, and perhaps Australia may have gone too far in this direction.

The magnitude of these cuts has lessened the extent to which exchange has to be used. The problem is one, mainly, of restoring equilibrium between costs and prices in export production. We need not consider the finer points of the purchasing power parity theory. In the end this theory merely focuses attention upon the balance of costs and prices in export production. Up to the end of 1932 this balance had not been restored and there were many arguments advanced in favour of a further depreciation of the currency. In particular, the Wallace Bruce Committee of April 1932 in its Report on a "Preliminary Survey of the Economic Problem" urged the following policy to restore balance between costs and prices:

In addition to greater efficiency under pressure of falling prices there are two methods of restoring balance—cutting costs and raising prices.

With the present trend of oversea prices, the cut in costs required to restore the balance if this way alone were followed would involve reductions in nominal wages and interest rates of the order of 50 per cent. The attempt to do this would threaten social and financial stability.

To attempt to restore export prices simply by raising the exchange would end in loss of control of the currency and general collapse.

There is, however, a probability that a solution can be found by using each method as far as is safe and practicable. The gap between export costs and prices is about 20 per cent. Some of this might be covered by direct cutting of costs, some by raising the exchange and some gained by increased efficiency throughout industry.

The re-absorption of all the unemployed is unattainable until prosperity is regained over a large part of the world. In the meantime the problem of relieving unemployment is pressing. But it is essential that the method of restoring equilibrium between costs and prices should be steadily pursued along with measures of alleviation, and that the latter should be framed so as not to impede but to form the basis of future prosperity.

This sums up admirably the nature of the policy of currency depreciation recommended to the Australian Government and the banking authorities from time to time. Fortunately, the pressure of economic circumstances forced this policy upon the authorities and it has been carried through with signal success.[1]

We have now to consider the administration of the policy.

VII. *A Sterling Exchange Standard*

By the end of 1930 the outside market for exchange was quoting the Australian pound at 15 % to 18 % depreciation on sterling compared with the Bank rate of $8\frac{1}{2}$% depreciation. Apart from the flight of capital then gathering force the main influence causing the depreciation in the outside market was the official effort to maintain a rate that over-valued Australian currency. With external aids an over-valuation of the currency can be sustained for a time, but in the circumstances of Australia in 1930 official policy was doomed to failure. Neither the banks nor the Government had the funds to meet the demands for London funds caused in part by over-valuing the currency. The banks were in fact heavily rationing their sales of London funds at the

---

[1] For the Report as a whole see Shann and Copland, *The Australian Price Structure*, p. 38. An earlier statement of the arguments for this middle course is given in my *Credit and Currency Control*, Chap. 6, and in the article by Giblin, Wood and Copland on "The Restoration of Economic Equilibrium" in *The Economic Record*, November 1930.

time. Consequently they lost business to the outside market, which became a much better register of the real value of Australian currency. In January 1931 the banks, following the step taken by the Bank of New South Wales in quoting rates more in harmony with the market rates, rapidly raised their exchange rates. By the end of the month the

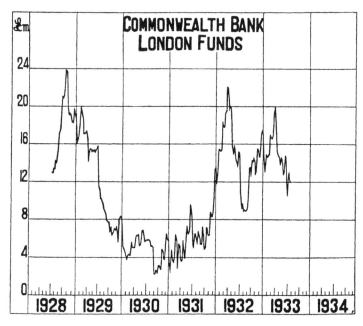

Chart 5

market and Bank rates were in close agreement at 23% depreciation on sterling. When the Premiers' Plan was adopted and the flight of capital checked there were fears that the rate might recede. In the absence of some international standard, or some controlling authority, short-period fluctuations in demand and supply of London funds were likely to cause rapid changes in the rate. This was all the more important in Australia where dealings in forward exchange were limited. At the opening of the export season the outside market was below £A. 130 for £stg. 100 and some banks were not buying freely. The difficulty was overcome by the Commonwealth Bank on December 3rd, 1931, assuming complete control. Unfortunately the Bank reduced the rate from 30% to 25% premium. No doubt the Bank was influenced in this decision by the depreciation of sterling. At the time Australian currency was depreciated approximately 40% in terms of gold. Since December 1931 the rate on sterling has remained at the figure fixed by the Bank. Thus Australia for the past two years has been operating a well-regulated sterling exchange standard with local currency at 20% depreciation on sterling. In normal times the operation of this standard requires

(i) That the Commonwealth Bank buys and sells exchange at fixed rates within prescribed limits.[1]

(ii) That the Bank holds a sufficient reserve of gold or foreign liquid assets to enable it to sell exchange freely, pending short period adjustments in the balance of payments.

(iii) That the Bank controls the currency and has the right to issue notes against sterling balances.

(iv) That the Bank has sufficient power and authority to modify internal banking policy to maintain the exchange parity agreed upon.

The Commonwealth Bank has been steadily moving towards the exercise of all these powers. The main steps taken up to the present were indicated in the last lecture.[2] I deal with the fourth of the above conditions in Lecture VII. The first and third are already in operation. What is the

---

[1] During the present period of transition the fixed rates might have to be altered until an equilibrium rate is found. For reasons given more fully in Lecture VII it might be desirable to make the limits wider than the old gold points.

[2] For a more complete account of the early steps see my *Credit and Currency Control*, Chap. 4.

position with regard to the second? A large reserve of gold or foreign liquid assets is essential to the maintenance of reasonable exchange stability in Australia. Short-period changes in both export prices and seasonal conditions are considerable, and a reserve is necessary to meet temporary shortage in the current supply of London funds. We have seen that before the depression these funds amounted to £95 m. in some years. With the export of £5 m. from the gold reserve to meet maturing treasury bills in London the reserves fell to below £stg. 30 m. at July 1st, 1931.[1] Since 1931 the external reserves of the Banking system in sterling values have benefited from the improved balance of trade, the return of capital to Australia and the transfer of Australian gold into sterling assets. On July 1st, 1932, bank balances in London were estimated at nearly £33 m. and the sterling value of gold reserves at £17 m., making a total of £50 m. No increase appears to have taken place in 1932/33, but short-term debt in London was reduced by £3 m.[2] It will be agreed that this figure is much too low and that every effort should be made to build up a substantially greater reserve abroad. Yet it is claimed in some quarters that the increase in London funds may depress the Australian exchange rate. In the past the rate has been held stable at parity with gold on many occasions when much larger accumulations of external reserves had to be handled. But there was then a belief in the stability of a rate at par with gold, and gold was the short-period regulating instrument. In the absence of gold we have

[1] This comprised an estimated amount of £14 m. banking funds and some £12 m. gold reserves compared with £47 m. and £48 m. of gold in 1928. For the method of estimating these banking balances see Wilson, *Capital Imports and the Terms of Trade*, p. 35.

[2] The Australian Banking system has freely sold its small gold reserves for sterling and has also held its sterling assets without thought of the future value of sterling. That is in contrast with the gold policy of some banking systems, even after suspension of gold payments. There is no reason why Australia should not exploit her independence by purchasing gold for reserves.

devised a new method of regulation through the Common-wealth Bank. It can proceed to build up very large London reserves. When they become sufficient to meet all likely short-period demands the Bank can promote an internal expansion of credit and spending power, which in the circumstances would be high as a consequence of high

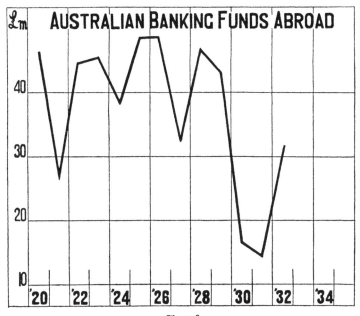

Chart 6

export prices. Imports would then expand and so use up some of the surplus London funds. The mechanism of this control must be left for discussion in Lecture VII.[1] Excess reserves could, if necessary, be used to liquidate short-term or even long-term debits in London. Thus an embarrassing

[1] Considerable research has been done in recent years on the relation of external banking reserves to internal banking policy and general economic conditions in Australia. See in particular Wilson, *Capital Imports, etc.*; Wood, *Borrowing and Business*; Copland, *Credit and Currency Control*; and articles by Isles and Wilson in *The Economic Record*, recent numbers.

accumulation of funds in London, an unlikely contingency at present, is easily handled by a strong central bank supported by a government determined to manage the currency with a view to promoting internal economic equilibrium and recovery.

This indeed is the present policy of the Australian Government. At the Premiers' Conference of April 1932 the Prime Minister strongly endorsed the proposals of the Committee referred to above, namely that the management of the exchange should be left to the Commonwealth Bank. The Bank, however, was to have special regard to economic conditions, and to the position of the export industries.[1] In June the Government secured the sanction of parliament for important amendments to the Commonwealth Bank Act permitting the issue of notes against sterling assets, and the transfer of gold reserves to sterling reserves. Any profit on this transaction was to be placed in a special reserve and could be used as a fund for stabilising or controlling exchange. To this extent the Bank could indemnify itself against losses incurred in exchange policy. In these circumstances the Bank could afford to stabilise the rate on sterling over considerable periods, but this rate must depend upon (a) the level of sterling itself, (b) the movement in Australian export prices, and (c) the cost level in Australian industry. A fixed relation to sterling is not at present the goal of exchange policy, though this might be the ultimate objective. The financial nexus with London is important; but it would be an error to make a fetish of stability with sterling, and still more of parity with sterling. Independent management of the currency requires that the rate of exchange should be such as to restore profit in industry at the level of costs that can be maintained without economic and

[1] The Prime Minister's statement is reproduced in Shann and Copland, *The Australian Price Structure*, pp. 95–7, together with important announcements by the Commonwealth Bank, and a second reference by the Prime Minister in the budget speech. See also Addendum below, p. 209.

social distress.[1] This equilibrium level can only be attained after experiment in much more settled world conditions than prevail at the moment. This experiment can be made only by the proper authorities in Australia continuing to pursue the cautious but independent course they have set themselves in the past three years. The final settlement of the rate of exchange must register the change in the terms of trade caused by the depression. If this is not done Australia will repeat the mistake made by Britain herself in 1925.

[1] The present level of costs might be described as a deflation level. It would be a mistake to accept it as one of the main guides to the fixation of the exchange. The price level as a whole would then tend to settle at from 20% to 25% below the pre-crisis level and this might make the debt structure top heavy. Some rise in export prices above the level required to restore balance between prices and present money costs would raise prices as a whole, expedite recovery and lighten the burden of debt.

VI

DEFLATIONARY ACTION—COSTS OF INDUSTRY AND PUBLIC EXPENDITURE

I. *Inflationary and Deflationary Action defined*

THE titles of this and the next lecture call for a word of explanation. Deflationary action is to be defined as action which reduces money incomes below the level in operation before the depression. Inflationary action is that which helps to sustain money incomes above the level they would tend to reach under the operation of a policy of adherence to an international gold standard. Strictly we should limit the use of inflation to those elements of economic policy that would cause the currency to depreciate in terms of domestic commodities. At a moment when prices in terms of the international standard are falling rapidly, action to shelter domestic commodities against this fall would not, in this restricted definition, be regarded as inflationary. Thus exchange depreciation of 40 % in terms of the international standard would not be inflationary if it left domestic commodities, as a whole, at lower prices in terms of domestic currency. Yet we could hardly designate exchange depreciation as deflationary. I have therefore thought it desirable to distinguish inflationary and deflationary action by reference to the effect of policy upon the relationship of the value of domestic currency in terms of commodities to that of the international standard. In the circumstances of the present depression, the idea of an international standard also raises difficulties. We must define this as the traditional gold standard, even though the standard at the moment is in operation in a comparatively small area of the world's currencies.

Inasmuch as the national income has fallen in terms of Australian currency, it would appear, at first sight, that the deflationary action has been of greater force than the inflationary action. We must remember, however, that the greatest deflationary force, viz. the fall in the external prices of exports, is not within the control of Australia. If the ultimate effect of Australian policy, as a whole, is to limit the appreciation of the Australian unit of currency in terms of commodities to less than one-half the appreciation of the international standard, we could not—in the light of our definition—say that a decline in the money value of Australian national income was evidence of the greater influence of deflationary action. Had we pursued a strict course of deflation, our adjustment would have been to a level of prices determined by the change in value of the international standard. We did not pursue this course, nor did we attempt to escape from depression by purely inflationary action within the terms of my definitions. We pursued a middle course between inflation and deflation. In this lecture I propose to examine the nature and influence of deflationary action. After dealing with the inflationary action in Lecture VII, I shall attempt to summarise the effects of a combination of the two sets of forces and to indicate the measures necessary to maintain a balance between them.

II. *The Attitude of the Arbitration Court*

In 1930 there was much emphasis upon the necessity for reducing costs. This indeed was the burden of Sir Otto Niemeyer's statement before the Premiers' Conference in August 1930. The following extract from his address indicates the nature of the advice he tendered:[1]

But there remains a more fundamental question on which, I believe, the above preliminary suggestions are ultimately

---

[1] Published in Shann and Copland, *The Crisis in Australian Finance*, p. 28.

conditioned. Australia cannot wish to remain for ever under a regime of emergency tariffs and rationed exchange. She has to emerge from that position and to show signs of progressing towards emergence. To achieve this end she depends inevitably to a large extent on the primary producer, and the power of the primary producer selling in the world market to assist depends very largely on the question of his costs, and those in turn depend very largely on the general costs in Australia, which govern what he has to pay for his supplies and services. I assume that everybody in this room is in agreement that costs must come down. There may be room for increased efficiency, but there seems to me little escape from the conclusion that in recent years Australian standards have been pushed too high relatively to Australian productivity and to general world conditions and tendencies.

This advice would, doubtless, have been accepted had it been accompanied by suggestions as to other forms of adjustment of what I have called an inflationary type that were open to Australia. There was little distinction between monetary and real costs, and monetary and real standards of living. Despite the formal agreement reached by the Governments at the Conference this policy was not officially adopted. We have to turn to a semi-official body, viz. the Arbitration Court, to get the first authoritative statement of the case for a reduction in costs. It is well to remember, however, that the Court itself hinted that its acceptance of the policy of reducing money costs was to be regarded as part of a general policy embracing both deflationary and inflationary action.[1]

After an exhaustive hearing the Arbitration Court de-

---

[1] Shann and Copland, *The Crisis in Australian Finance.* It is worth noting that the policy of deflation was still being strongly recommended to the Governments in February 1931, after the Court's declaration. Thus the Report of the Committee of Under-Treasurers to the Loan Council in February 1931 was severely deflationist. The following brief extract on the effects of a high exchange rate will illustrate the point: "The high rate of exchange, through its effect in raising import prices and the local prices of exports, counteracts the readjustment to lower costs, and must in the long run offset that readjustment. Thus a high rate of exchange is of little or no permanent benefit to the exporter".

livered its important judgment on January 22nd, 1931. It ordered a reduction in the real basic wage of 10% and maintained the quarterly adjustment of the wage rate to movements in the cost of living as measured by an index number covering food, groceries and house rent. At the outset the Court intimated that it had been prepared then, as in the past, "to entertain applications to vary awards on the ground of substantial change in economic conditions".

Though the general effect of the Court's decisions in the past had been to raise wage rates above the level operating before the Harvester judgment (1907), and to apply these standards to many industries not hitherto falling under the jurisdiction of wage-fixing tribunals, the Court had not ignored the economic conditions operating in the country as a whole or in the particular industries. Nevertheless, there is evidence to show, as was indicated in Lecture I, that the basic wage had reached an uneconomic level prior to the depression. With the heavy loss of income caused by the depression, the Court was impressed by the fundamental change in the economic position. After giving an estimate of the loss, the judgment proceeds:[1]

> The Court's difficulty was to get the respondents to realise the actuality and alarming extent of this fall in the community's spending power. Some of the decline is undoubtedly psychological in origin. The prevailing air of uncertainty, the precarious state of public finance and continuance of fall in price levels, local ànd universal, are responsible for much of the commercial and industrial stagnation. But taking the most optimistic view, it is clear that the bulk of the lost spending power is a harsh reality, and the restoration of the customary value of our productivity will be a long and laborious process.

III. *Wages and Spending Power*

The Court, however, had to be assured that a reduction in the wage rate would expedite the task of economic readjustment. The argument was advanced that a reduction

[1] The judgment is published in *The Crisis in Australian Finance*, pp. 102–46.

in wages, by causing a decline in consumers' spending power, would aggravate rather than mitigate the depression. The Court met this argument by considering the effect of the transfer of income that would follow the reduction in the wage rate. The Court's view, to quote again from the judgment, was as follows:[1]

Let us assume that the reduction has been made and that the corresponding amount of spending power has been transferred. The transferred spending power will be used by the employers, or by those to whom it may be assigned by the employers, either in employing other labour or in the purchase of goods or services which may be necessaries or luxuries or capital goods, but as to all of which the production, in the long run, is achieved by the employment of labour. The labour thus employed ultimately in Australia by means of the transferred spending power may not be used in the production of goods or services so necessary to wage-earners in the aggregate or to the community as those that would have been produced if the spending power had not been transferred; if this be so it would be objectionable, but on other grounds than a lessening of employment. Only to the extent that the spending power is as a result of the transfer more used abroad would the total amount of employment in Australia procured by the spending power be diminished by the transfer.

This argument may be challenged on the ground that it ignores the possible effects upon credit policy and savings of a reduction in wage rates. Suppose that the whole of the savings in wages are devoted by employers to liquidation of debt. In this case there would be a heavy contraction of credit and a net decline in spending power. In these circumstances, the reduction in wages would intensify the depression. But these were not the circumstances which the Court itself contemplated. After summarising the views of economists and others who urged an expansion of credit and a rise in exchange as necessary features of a comprehensive economic policy embracing also reductions in money costs, the Court remarked: "The consensus of

[1] *The Crisis in Australian Finance*, p. 125.

opinion, however, is that some change in the direction of granting facilities to increase credits is necessary". Unfortunately, the Court's decision was put into effect some time before other elements of economic policy were agreed upon. In particular, the budgetary adjustment and the partial restoration of public investment were not in progress for a full six months after the wage rate had been reduced. Moreover, in New South Wales the wage rate declared by the State Industrial Court was not reduced until August 1932. In these circumstances, it is futile to judge the effects of the reduction in the Commonwealth basic wage by reference to the economic conditions of 1931. Other forces were in operation tending to upset the general assumptions made by the Court in its argument that spending power would be transferred and not side tracked into the liquidation of debt.

Another feature of the Court's judgment is of special interest. Agreeing with the view that the Harvester standard of 1907 was about 25% higher than that which operated prior to that date, the Court expressed the opinion that the maintenance of the Harvester rate would not necessarily provide the workers with a proper share of production in 1931. The Court was, in fact, greatly influenced by the argument that a spreading of the loss of income was a condition of economic recovery. On this point, the following extract from the judgment will indicate the attitude of the Court:

The only chance of maintaining the past average quantitative production of primary products is by reduction of production costs. Wool at 8*d*. per lb., and wheat at 2*s*. 6*d*. per bushel, do not leave producers any margin above present costs of production. However prosperous these classes of the community may have been during recent years, they are now in a parlous state. The value of their assets has greatly declined, whilst their fixed charges, such as interest, railway freights, etc., remain at a high level. The primary producer, unless there is some increase in prices, of which there is at present not the faintest indication, must be enabled to produce at lower costs. He must pay less for his machinery and plant, his fertilizers, his use of capital and his labour, or go out of production. The State, of course, up to a point may assist him and, while it lasts, the adverse exchange rate is in his favour. But in the present state of public finance there is a limit to the assistance the State can give, and the adverse exchange rate cannot be accepted as a permanent form of relief to those who export products. That the primary producer is carrying more than his share of the burden cannot be disputed.

It was not, of course, the business of the Court to deal with the distribution of the loss of income as a whole. In as far as the share going to the wage-earners in employment was excessive the Court could take action to correct it. Believing that reduction in costs was necessary for the maintenance of export production the Court was able to justify its decision on the ground that relief would be afforded to the export producer who was carrying an undue share of the loss of income.

This argument, as indicated in Lecture III, has great weight in Australia. Export production plays a predominant part in determining the amount and nature of the national income. If exporters' incomes are low, their capacity to purchase goods from sheltered and protected production will be correspondingly reduced. If the prices of the latter goods do not decline the quantity purchased by exporters will fall, and unemployment will be serious in sheltered and protected production. Any decline in costs and prices of sheltered and protected goods will increase real spending power of exporters, and ultimately help to restore the volume of sheltered and protected production. Thus a reduction in wages that allows a fall of prices in sheltered and protected industries must ultimately help to expand employment. It is possible, however, that with a progressive reduction in the volume of investment and an increase in savings, unemployment may actually increase even though a fall in price accompanies the wage reduction. To some extent this was happening in Australia in 1931. Investment as a whole had declined throughout 1930 and was at its lowest point in the latter half of 1931. The decline in public investment (loan expenditure) is indicated in the following table:

Year	Common-wealth	State	Total
	£,000	£,000	£,000
1928/29	8,231	33,096	41,327
1929/30	5,292	24,538	29,830
1930/31	1,989	15,986	17,975
1931/32	3,450	7,112	10,562

Apart from other manufactures, the following industrial groups showed unemployment in the third quarter of 1931 at a higher level than the average unemployment— building, engineering, mining, quarrying, etc. These are, in the main, the heavy industries, and their greater incidence of unemployment may be regarded as evidence of the slump in investment. It cannot be argued that the reduction in the basic wage was a deterrent to investment. On the contrary, it did in the long run encourage investment. Nor, as we have shown, can it be argued that a net decline in consumers' income would necessarily follow a reduction in wages. In the special circumstances of Australia, and on the assumptions the Court seems to have made, its argument that a reduction in the basic wage would migitate the depression must be conceded as being valid.

IV. *Disparities in Wage Rates*

The lead given by the Commonwealth Court was not followed by all the State tribunals. The Commonwealth basic wage fell by nearly 30 % in nominal value between

1928 and the second quarter of 1932 while the real value of the wage had fallen 8%. On the 1929 standard, which was higher on account of the rise in the cost of living in that year, the decline was approximately 10%. In its award of May 1933 the Court accepted the "all items" index number of the cost of living, which includes clothing and miscellaneous expenditure, for the purpose of bringing the real basic wage to a level approximately 10% below the 1929 standard. On account of the relatively greater fall in food prices, the use of the index number covering only food, groceries and house rents tended to reduce the real basic wage by more than 10% below the 1929 level.

For State awards the adjustment in the basic wage has been far from uniform. The changes in nominal and real basic wages from 1928 to the second quarter of 1933 were as follows:

	Nominal	Real
New South Wales	Fall 24%	Fall 2%
Queensland	„ 13%	Rise 6%
Southern Australia	„ 26%	„ 6%
Western Australia	„ 18%	„ 9%

The basic wage in New South Wales was £4. 5s. 6d. in 1928 for a man and wife. Child allowance was paid at the rate of 5s. per child. In 1929 the family unit was altered and the basic wage fixed at £4. 2s. 6d. for a man, wife and one child. This unit has been used since and its effect is to cause a greater reduction in the nominal wage than the crude figures suggest. Using the crude figure the reduction is from 85s. in 1928 to 68s. 6d. in the second quarter of this year, namely 20%. If, however, we add 5s. to the basic wage for 1928 to allow for the change in unit the nominal basic wage in New South Wales has fallen by 24%, as shown in the foregoing table. In South Australia the fall in the cost of living has been so heavy that a reduction of 26% in nominal wages is accompanied by a rise of 6% in real wages. In the other two States the adjustment in the basic wage does not nearly satisfy the standard set by the Commonwealth Court. The difference between the basic

Chart 7

wages fixed in the capital cities by Commonwealth and State tribunals in May 1933 is shown in the following table:

NOMINAL BASIC WAGES

	Commonwealth Court			State Court		
	£	s.	d.	£	s.	d.
Sydney	3	7	10	3	8	6
Brisbane	2	19	4	3	14	0
Adelaide	2	19	2	3	3	0
Perth	2	19	9	3	9	0

In Victoria and Tasmania the tendency is for wages fixed by the wages boards to conform to Commonwealth standards. The differences are most marked in Queensland and Western Australia, but in New South Wales there is also a substantial difference for rates payable to men with more than one child. These differences in wage rates have been the subject of special comment by the Commonwealth Court. In its award of May 5th, 1933 in the basic wage case the Court estimated that about 50 % of the total workers of the Commonwealth had experienced a reduction of approximately 10 % in real wages. The Court feared that wage earners would seek to avoid the reduction by approaching the more favourable State tribunals. "Action on these lines has already commenced, and it appears likely from the information which is available to the Court, to be an accelerated movement in the near future." The Court regretted that it had no power to rectify the anomaly.[1] Owing to divergences in practice concerning the basic wage, and no doubt also to differences in adjustments of margins for skill, the nominal wage rate as a whole for Australia fell from 100 in 1928 to 81·4 in the fourth quarter of 1932, the latest date for which these index numbers are available. This meant an increase of 5 % in the real wage on the 1928 standard. Hence the effort of the Commonwealth Court to adjust wages on a common basis of 10 % reduction in real wages has by no means succeeded. But a fall of nearly 20 % in nominal wages over the whole field

[1] The Court rejected in the following statement the plea for upward revision of its own standards in order to restore uniformity: "Having regard to the position indicated above, the Court is driven to the necessity of asking itself whether the evil of differential rates for the same classes of employment, brought about by State tribunals and State legislatures refusing to conform to the lowered standards regarded as essential by this Court, is greater than the evil that would attend the restoration of the former standards in the Federal sphere until such time as the legislatures shall have taken common action to secure uniformity in any reduction found to be necessary on economic grounds. In our view, having regard to all the facts indicated above and in the several previous judgments of the Court on the same subject matter, there is no present justification for a general restoration of those standards".

of wage earners in a period of three years is a substantial adjustment. The very heavy decline in retail prices, amounting to more than 25 % at the end of 1932 and 27 % by the middle of 1933, explains the rise in real wages. All wages are not subject to automatic adjustment to changes in the cost of living and in a period of declining prices it is usual for a pronounced rise in real wages to take place. With a recovery in retail prices wages not subject to automatic adjustment will fall in real value. This aspect of the wage problem, as well as the differences in rates, was the subject of special consideration by the Wallace Bruce Committee in April 1932. Urging a common cut of 10 % in real wages as necessary the Committee pointed out that "the required fall in nominal wages would be made less severe by a rise in the rate of exchange setting in operation forces tending to raise all prices, and thus to offset the fall in prices resulting from lower wages. We should have attained the lower level of wages with a steadier level of prices".[1]

This suggests that the deflation caused by the heavy fall in export prices had been too severe for a swift adjustment of all wages to the standard set by the Commonwealth Court. Making allowance for the unwillingness of certain States to expedite the reduction in wages, or to carry it as far as the Commonwealth Court desired, the view is probably sound. Had the deflation been less severe the reduction in real wages would have been greater and more uniformly applied. But any recovery in retail prices will almost certainly be accompanied by some reduction in real wages as a whole, though happily not in wages fixed by the Commonwealth Court.

It is one of the advantages of the system of wage fixation in Australia that the wage rate can be adjusted rapidly to changing economic conditions. The problems raised by dis-

[1] Report, par. 64.

parities in wage rates fixed by different tribunals are less
acute than in Great Britain where the sheltered industries
have been able, over long periods, to maintain wages considerably in excess of the wages paid in the export industries.
Pending a recovery in export prices this problem did, however, exist in Australia, for pastoral awards were in some

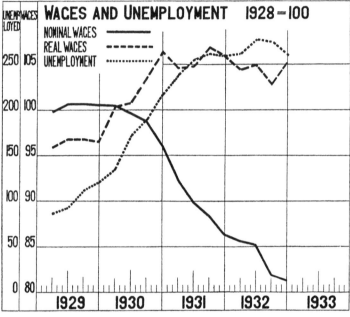

Chart 8

cases suspended and wage rates declined more than the
average. Despite this disparity it must be regarded as a
considerable achievement that the wage rates in sheltered
industries coming under the Commonwealth Court could
be reduced rapidly by 25 % without industrial disturbance.
The wage structure was therefore flexible and the special
claims of ability to pay in individual industries had much
less weight than the general ability of the country to pay a

given rate of wages. By thus expediting a general and equitable distribution of the share of the loss of income falling on wage-earners, the decision of the Court was a major influence promoting economic adjustment.

V. *The Basis of Budget Adjustment*

The Court's decision was accepted as impartial and reasonable in the circumstances and it became the basis of the general adjustment in Government expenditure and fixed charges imposed by the Premiers' Plan. In February 1931 the Committee of Under-Treasurers in their report to the Loan Council estimated the aggregate deficits for 1930/31 at £15 m. On the basis of taxation and expenditure then in operation the Committee forecasted a deficit of not less than £25 m. for 1931/32.[1]

Unfortunately the decline in national income was proceeding so rapidly that the government revenue was falling away at a greater rate than was generally realised. Moreover, the provision of unemployment expenditure and the depreciation of the currency increased the disbursements of governments and rendered ineffective the economies that were then in operation. The governments were obtaining financial assistance from the Commonwealth Bank, but on April 2nd, 1931 the Chairman of the Commonwealth Bank advised the Chairman of the Loan Council that the Bank could not provide further assistance to the governments. It limited its advances to a total of £25 m. within Australia and £25,125,000 abroad. The latter figure had already been reached. The internal advances made by the Bank at that date were £19 m. In these circumstances, the finance available for governments would be exhausted within two

[1] Report published in *The Crisis in Australian Finance*. This was a document containing much detailed information upon government expenditure and the general economic position. It emphasised the importance of a reduction in expenditure but did not show how the budget could be balanced by this means alone.

months. The Chairman's letter is of great significance in that it forced the Loan Council to take careful stock of the budgetary position. The result was the appointment of a sub-committee of the Council to consider what action must be taken to secure a balanced budget at the end of June 1934. This sub-committee had power to co-opt the services of "economists and such other advisors as it may deem fit". The result was the formation of a committee of four economists and five under-treasurers (the Copland Committee). It was the report of this committee that laid the basis of budgetary reform and the Premiers' Plan.

The Committee found the budgetary position to be much worse than the February committee had suggested. The estimated deficits for 1930/31 were put at £31 m. and the forecast for 1931/32 from £39 to £41 m. In considering the methods to be adopted to bridge this wide gap in the budgets the committee considered three questions:

(a) What further economies were possible?

(b) What increases in revenue could be gained from taxation or other source?

(c) If these failed to meet the probable deficit, what further measures were necessary?[1]

It is impossible here to review in detail the report, important though it be. Accepting the decision of the Commonwealth Court as a standard for economy, the committee found that pending general economic recovery the possible reductions in expenditure on this basis, together with the possible increases in revenue, left a gap in the budget too wide to be met by borrowing. A slight examination of the budgetary position will demonstrate the difficulties of balancing the budgets by the traditional method of economy, plus additional taxation. On this basis, certain expenditure must be regarded as non-adjustable. Thus

[1] The Report is published in Shann and Copland, *The Battle of the Plans*, pp. 75–107

interest and sinking funds on the debt are within this category. In view of the importance of the depreciation of the currency, exchange was added to non-adjustable expenditure. Finally, the provision for unemployment in a depression must be regarded also as non-adjustable. The total of these non-adjustable items amounted to nearly £80 m. in 1931 out of an expenditure of less than £190 m. when Commonwealth grants to the States are deducted from State expenditure. This left an adjustable expenditure of about £110 m. on which savings of, approximately, £40 m. for 1931/32 had to be made. In these circumstances something more drastic than a reduction in salaries, wages, pensions and other allowances was called for. On this point, it will be desirable to quote at some length from the report of the Copland Committee.

36. Economies and increased taxes such as those outlined above involve as drastic cuts as can be borne by income-elements that are exposed to both cuts and taxes. Yet the gap still to be bridged remains a wide one. For two reasons, further measures to reduce it are necessary. The sacrifices asked from wages, salaries, and pensions are so great that they would not be accepted if any other income-element escaped. Nor may the menace of currency collapse be ignored while the deficit to be met by borrowing remains so large.

37. The holders of fixed money-claims have already borne taxation as part of a special Commonwealth tax on property of 1s. 6d. in the £1 (7½ per cent.) and may have suffered reduction of such income as they derive from other sources. But their incomes from fixed money-claims have not been reduced to the same degree as other income-elements. Outstanding amongst them, from the point of view of the public finance, are the holders of government securities, for whom the danger inherent in unbalanced budgets carries its gravest threat.

38. This threat affects most directly the internal bondholder. Measures that will obviate it must therefore include him, but they must leave untouched the external creditor. The external creditor has not the responsibility for the financial position which every Australian citizen must share. Moreover,

default or attempts to vary the contracts with external creditors would rob us of assistance that is necessary, both in preventing collapse and in opening the road to recovery.

39. There are two methods by which, without a technical breach of contract, contributions might be exacted from internal holders of fixed money-claims. One is that of raising the price level either by the issue of additional currency or by the creation of bank credit. There can be little doubt that under present conditions such a policy would destroy confidence in the currency. With such loss of confidence both interest and exchange rates would rise. The rise in exchange would increase the cost of meeting overseas interest obligations and therefore upset the whole plan for budget equilibrium. The increase in interest rates would be damaging to conversion operations and again impose an additional strain upon the Budget. The net effect would be to increase the deficit and to require an increasing amount of new credit and currency to be created for balancing the budgets in successive years. In these circumstances an inflationary policy would soon get out of hand and bring about a collapse of the currency.

The second method referred to in paragraph 39 of the report was the special taxation of income from fixed money-claims. This was rejected on the ground that it would raise the rate of interest, render future conversion loans difficult and impose heavy burdens upon export production. The committee, therefore, considered other methods of reducing the burden of interest upon the budget. These methods, however, involved a breach of contract, but this did not deter the committee from recommending the adoption of one of them, a recommendation that was justified in the following passage taken from the report:

In normal times breach of contract would constitute an insuperable objection, but, fundamental as is the sanctity of contracts, it must not be overlooked that insistence on their fulfilment to the letter might, in present circumstances, force the debtor Government into a policy that would surely destroy the value of the bond. Generally, breach of contract would cause lack of confidence, and would set up a flight of capital from the country subjecting investors to it. But when the alternatives are inflation and default, or taxation of an equal or probably greater severity, holders of fixed money-claims may find it wiser to accept a variation of their contracts which is less onerous than taxation and insures them against the greater loss of total default.

One of the methods suggested by the committee was the conversion of the internal debt to a lower rate of interest. This conversion was to be accompanied by "a simultaneous reduction of bank interest rates and mortgage rates".

VI. *The Premiers' Plan*

The report was, in general, adopted by the Premiers' Conference that followed and became the Premiers' Plan. Only in one major particular did the Premiers' Plan depart from the report of the Copland Committee. It was suggested by the latter that the wage adjustment carried out by the Arbitration Court should be extended to all wages, just as the proposed reduction in interest on the public debt should be extended to private interest. The Premiers' Plan ignored the wage adjustment, leaving it to the State Industrial Tribunals. In the report of the Premiers' Conference, the Plan was stated as follows:

The Conference has, therefore, adopted a plan which combines all possible remedies in such a way that the burden falls as equally as possible on every one, and no considerable section of the people is left in a privileged position. This sharing of the burden is necessary to make the load more tolerable; it is still more necessary, because only on this condition will it be possible to get the combined effort required. The plan has been adopted by the Conference as a whole, each part of which is accepted on the understanding that all the other parts are equally and simultaneously put into operation. It embraces the following measures:

(*a*) A reduction of 20 per cent. in all adjustable government expenditure, as compared with the year ending 30th June 1930, including all emoluments, wages, salaries, and pensions paid by the Governments, whether fixed by statute or otherwise, such reduction to be equitably effected;

(*b*) Conversion of the internal debts of the Governments on the basis of a 22½ per cent. reduction of interest;

(*c*) The securing of additional revenue by taxation, both Commonwealth and State;

(*d*) A reduction of bank and Savings Bank rates of interest on deposits and advances;

(*e*) Relief in respect of private mortgages.

These proposals require the greatest effort in economy and taxation which the Conference considers it safe to attempt. The effect will be still to have a gap of from £13,000,000 to £15,000,000 to be covered for a time by borrowing.

The decision to reduce interest on the internal debt by $22\frac{1}{2}\%$ requires a word of explanation. The Copland Committee had suggested a reduction of 15 % in interest because at that time a special tax of $7\frac{1}{2}\%$ had been levied on income from interest. The Premiers' Conference decided to lift this special tax on interest on the internal debt and to bring about a reduction of $22\frac{1}{2}\%$ in interest.

The legislation required to implement the Plan consisted of the following:[1]

1. A Debt Conversion Agreement Act passed by the Commonwealth and by the States approving an agreement under Section 105A of the Commonwealth Constitution, between the States and the Commonwealth, relative to the conversion of the internal debt.

2. An Act to provide for the conversion of the internal debts passed by the Commonwealth Government.

3. An Act passed by all parliaments to empower trustees to convert their holding of the public debt into the new loan.

4. A Financial Bill embodying the reductions in Government expenditure, and in some cases also the reductions in private interest.

5. An increase in taxation in the Commonwealth raising the income tax, the primage duty and the sales tax to provide revenue amounting to £7,500,000.

---

[1] The remainder of this Section reproduced substantially as given in an article contributed to *The Economic Journal*, December 1931.

The important features of this legislation are the terms of the conversion of the internal debt and the provisions for reducing private interest. With regard to the first, the total amount involved was £556 m., on which the average rate of interest was £5. 5s. 5d. per cent. at June 30th, 1930. Under the conversion loan this rate was reduced to an average of £4. 1s. 8d. per cent., a reduction of 22½ per cent. The gross savings in interest were £6½ m. The conversion operation had another advantage. It was possible to re-arrange the maturity dates of the internal debt. Holdings of the existing securities were allocated among new 4% securities whose dates of maturity ranged from seven years in nine steps to thirty years. This left the local market free of conversion operations for seven years, and spread the conversions more conveniently over the remaining twenty-three years. The Act provided that unless dissent was signified, conversion would be automatic. Bond-holders were appealed to on the double ground of the financial difficulties of the governments and on the need for sacrifice from every section of the community. The result was re-markable. No less than 97 per cent. of the total holdings were converted into the new loan, leaving only £17·5 m. unconverted. With concessions to hard cases this amount was later compulsorily converted.

With regard to private interest, legislation was to be passed in the six States providing for a reduction of 22½ per cent. on existing contracts.[1] No attempt was to be made to control the future rate of interest, and it was left open to the States to legislate on their own plan. Four of the States (New South Wales, Victoria, Western Australia and Tasmania) proceeded by way of automatic reduction, unless the mortgagee could satisfy a tribunal that the reduction

---

[1] I append to this lecture a statement on the legal principles involved in this legislation and in the moratorium legislation. For this statement I am indebted to Mr J. G. Norris, LL.M., Lecturer in Commercial Law in the University of Melbourne.

was inequitable. In the other two States the mortgagor must apply for a reduction. Rates were reduced by 22½ per cent. with a minimum in most cases of 5 per cent. For the most part bank rates were omitted from the plan, inasmuch as the banks had already agreed to a reduction of 1 per cent. all round in their deposit rates and advances rates.

The reductions in expenditure were on the whole on a greater scale than those contemplated in the Plan, amounting to nearly 30% of the adjustable expenditure in some States. Despite the savings involved in these economies and the net reduction of interest, the budget deficits were larger than anticipated in the Plan. The explanation lies in the continued decline in export prices and the fall in national income in 1931/32 below the level anticipated when the Plan was formulated. Export prices, in fact, declined by 12% from the middle of 1931 to the end of 1932 and government revenue was consequently lower. The amount of the deficits, the method by which they were financed and the effects of this on banking policy will be considered in the next lecture.

VII. *Constructive Deflation*

Legislation forcing a reduction of interest both public and private may be justified on grounds of grave economic necessity. With the fall in national income, fixed charges (public interest, mortgage interest, rents) had become too burdensome. Whether it was desirable to allow reductions to be made piecemeal by the pressure of economic distress will remain a matter for discussion for some time. The problem was hotly debated during the formulation of the Premiers' Plan and subsequently during the parliamentary discussions on the legislation. The case for special and ordered action was stated by the Copland Committee in the extract quoted above (p. 132). Apart from the immediate legal problems involved, and the technical breach of contract, there is the interesting question of the ultimate economic effects. It was argued that action of the kind taken destroyed the security of future investments, and was contrary to accepted economic principles. This would certainly have been true had the State acted capriciously. But surely this was not the case. I am not competent to discuss all the legal aspects of the problem. On economic grounds, however, it must be recognised that the depression had altered the basis of contracts. The increase in the value of money, and the reduced capacity of the debtor to pay, demanded some modification of contracts, if solvency were to be preserved and recovery to be expedited. But the alteration of the contracts was designed to reduce fixed charges by an amount proportional to the appreciation of the value of money, plus the loss of real income that was to be imposed upon the creditor in common with other members of the community. Special arguments that the creditor was not a member of a clearly defined group, that he was sometimes less able to suffer a loss of income than the debtor, or that he was gravely embarrassed by the reduction in income, did not affect the main issue. Cases of hardship existed among wage-earners, farmers, government officials. There was in fact no special discrimination against the creditor.

No effort was made to regulate the rate of interest or rents in the future. The legislation was designed to adjust existing contracts to the changed economic conditions. For the future, interest and rent were to be fixed by the parties concerned under the normal conditions of market rates. It is argued, however, that a dangerous precedent has been established and that similar action should be taken to raise fixed charges should prices rise rapidly and debtors' capacity to pay increase under a policy of inflation. On the first point the only comment to be made is that a capricious alteration of contracts by the State would certainly destroy the basis of existing economic society. There is no precedent for this in the action taken by Australia in 1931 to adjust fixed charges to the fall in national income and the rise in the value of money. On the second point, it is only necessary to draw attention to the proposals of economists for a tabular standard or a more stable price level. Until the problem of reasonable stability in the price level has been solved, the use of some form of tabular standard would overcome the injustices suffered by both debtors and creditors by the payment of fixed charges in a unit of currency that fluctuates in value.

Fears that arbitrary action to reduce fixed charges would raise the rate of interest, reduce savings and cause a scarcity of capital, have not been justified. The new 4% consolidated Commonwealth Stock now bears an effective rate of interest of less than $3\frac{3}{4}$% compared with over $5\frac{1}{2}$% when the stock was first quoted on the Stock Exchange. The treasury bill rate is $2\frac{1}{2}$% compared with 4% in 1931. Mortgage finance is available at rates below those ruling in 1929 and banks, pastoral companies and financial institutions generally now lend at lower rates. Savings are increasing and there has been no flight of capital. On the contrary capital has returned to Australia since the Premiers' Plan, with its compulsory reduction of interest, was promulgated. These favourable developments may not be regarded as the economic consequences of the revision of contracts. They are, as we shall see in the next lecture, partly a result of banking policy, and partly a natural movement in conditions where the investment is not profitable at higher rates of interest. They at least show that no fundamental economic principle was contravened by the special action taken in 1931. It was the current notion of economic principle that was offended, and not the real principle. For there is no authority in economic literature for the strict financial interpretation of the doctrine: *fiat justitia, ruat caelum.* Justice cannot be done by forcing payment in a currency that is so appreciated as to destroy or greatly to reduce capacity to pay. Australia was acting prudently in revising contracts on the principle that the real meaning of the contract itself had been altered by the rapid economic changes forced upon her in the depression. Interference with contract, in these circumstances, was an integral element of a constructive policy. Deflation was applied to all incomes with the object of correcting a distortion in the cost and price structure by spreading quickly and equitably the loss of real income. We may legitimately designate this as *constructive deflation* in contrast to the type of deflation that attacks certain incomes only, and thus adds to the disparity in real incomes among different classes. The deflationary policy pursued by Australia had the additional merit that it was accompanied by certain inflationary action. We proceed in the next lecture to consider the nature and effects of this aspect of Australian policy.

VIII. *The Interest Reduction and Moratorium Legislation*
(Prepared by Mr J. G. Norris, LL.M.)

In order that the plan might be carried into effect so far as obligations other than those constituted by the loan of money to governments were concerned, it was necessary that legislation should be enacted by the various States of the Commonwealth of Australia. It must be remembered that Australia is a Federation established under the authority of an Imperial Statute—the Commonwealth of Australia Constitution Act (63 and 64 Victoria, Cap. 12). The Commonwealth Parliament is entrusted with legislative power in respect of certain specified matters, only the residuum of legislative power being vested in the respective parliaments of the several States. The law of obligations generally is a matter in respect of which the Commonwealth Parliament has no power to legislate.

In these circumstances, the legislation which effectuated the plan is rather complex. Rough drafts of statutory provisions that would, it was thought, achieve the desired result were prepared by the legal advisers of the representatives of the governments at the Premiers' Conference, but upon consideration they were found by most States to be inadequate. Accordingly, one does not find a series of statutes in identical terms passed by all State legislatures. Rather, the position is that each State set about solving the problem in its own way and paid no very great regard to what was being done in the others. It is therefore impracticable to give more than a general description, so far as it is possible, of the principles upon which the legislation was framed.

The matter has two aspects, the first being concerned with the reduction of interest, the second with the creation of a moratorium. To these must be added a consideration of the nature and extent of the obligations which were sought to be affected by the legislation. The reduction of interest was achieved by either of two methods. In New South Wales, Victoria, Western Australia and Tasmania it was provided that the reduction should be automatic on the passing of the legislation, subject, however, to a right in the creditor to apply to the Courts for an order in his particular case excluding or modifying the reduction. The conditions of his obtaining such an order vary, but, to a great extent, the Courts were given an unhampered discretion to do as they thought fit. In the exercise of this discretion the Courts appear to have realised that the legislation was directed to the achievement of a general economic purpose, and have not exercised their discretion upon a mere consideration of the relative financial positions of creditor and debtor. For instance, the Full Court of Victoria in *Buckley* v. *The Myer Emporium Ltd.* (*1932*), *V.L.R. 268*, refused to make an order excluding or modifying the reduction of interest at the instance of a holder of one of a series of debentures over the assets of a large company, despite the fact that the company was paying an average dividend to shareholders of 6·2% and had large reserves, while the debenture holder's interest was being reduced from 6½% to about 5% by virtue of the statutory reduction. The period for which the reduction of interest is to continue in force varies also. For instance, in Victoria it is to continue in force during such part of the term of the obligation as falls within the period of three years from the 1st October, 1931 when the Victorian Financial Emergency Act came into operation. In New South Wales the reduction continues in force during the continuance of the obligation.

In Queensland and South Australia the legislation was less kind to the debtor. It required him to apply to the Courts for a reduction of his interest, and he had to advance reasons for the making of the order. The Queensland Financial Emergency Act 1921 declared that the Court might reduce interest if special circumstances were shown. The Court was not, to any real extent, restricted in determining what those special circumstances were to be. In South Australia, again, the debtor had to show special circumstances to obtain the interest reduction. The Queensland reduction continues in force during the continuance of the obligation, while orders made in South Australia are, in the first instance, in operation limited to three years at the most.

We turn now to the Moratorium provisions. The Statutes here fall into two main categories. You have Moratorium Acts of general application and Statutes in the nature of debt adjustment Acts, passed for the benefit of the farming community. The Moratorium Acts, properly so-called, deal with the problem again in either of two ways. In New South Wales, Western Australia and Tasmania the Acts provide that the creditor shall not exercise any of his remedies for realising on his security or otherwise for obtaining payment of the moneys owing to him, unless he gets the leave of the Court, which he must himself seek. The conditions on which he may obtain such leave vary greatly, and it is not desirable here to go into particulars as to them. In Victoria, Queensland and South Australia, the onus was cast upon the debtor of seeking an order from the Courts restricting the exercise by the mortgagee of his remedies. The conditions of obtaining the order again vary to a great extent, but the wide discretion that was entrusted to the Court in excluding or modifying interest reductions is here not to be found. The Court is bound on proof of the existence of the specified conditions to make the order restricting the exercise by the mortgagee of his remedies.

The Debt Adjustment Acts generally prescribe for some degree of protection from legal actions to be obtained by the farmer, while his assets are applied to the satisfaction of his debts in a prescribed order of priority. Provision is usually made for the payment to the farmer of a living allowance in the first instance.[1]

As for the obligations which are subject to the operation of the moratorium and the interest reductions, they again vary from State to State. For instance, in New South

[1] Debt adjustment and farmers' relief have been the subject of special legislation in most States. The legislation in South Australia and Western Australia is described in articles by Messrs F. S. Alford and S. E. Solomon in *The Economic Record*, December 1932. For the legislation in New South Wales see Mr F. A. Bland's article in *The Economic Record*, June 1933. Concerning the New South Wales Act, Mr Bland remarks that it breaks new ground by combining the principle of moratorium legislation with a plan for positive assistance by the State towards rehabilitation. "It is a drastic measure, because it deprives the farmer of his financial independence, but it affords the possibility of recovery as against the alternative of complete bankruptcy." The Act provides a Farm Relief Board which appoints a "supervisor" who assumes the management of the finances of a farmer and controls and handles his moneys. The Act applies to farmers who within twelve months of its proclamation ask to come under its provisions. The Board has power to make advances for the maintenance of the farmer and his family or to guarantee his purchases or assist him in purchasing necessary supplies. The maximum rate of interest charged on advances under these provisions is 4%. D. B. C.

Wales, the reduction of interest is applicable to all obligations to pay interest, subject to certain specified exceptions. Generally, however, moratorium and interest reductions alike apply to the same obligations. These are generally termed in the Act "mortgages" and the definition of mortgage is based upon the common principle of including any agreement whereby security is granted over real or personal property for the payment of money. This is wide enough but particular extensions, based on no principle, are made in particular cases. New South Wales reduces dividends on preference shares, while most States include in the definition contracts for the sale of land under which interest is payable on the purchase money. This is a wide extension, the conveyancing practice in Australia being to have long term contracts for the sale of land rather than a conveyance to the purchaser on paying his first instalment of purchase and leaving the balance on mortgage to the vendor. Hire purchase agreements and many other common commercial transactions are also included.

Contracting out of the legislation has of course not been allowed at any rate so far as agreements made prior to the passing of the legislation are concerned, while legislative amendments have from time to time extended the ambit of the prohibition.

NOTE. In 1816 J. R. McCulloch in *An Essay on the Question of Reducing the Interest on the National Debt* urged that interest reduction was a necessary part of deflation. "We must either reduce the interest of the national debt, which impartial justice and sound policy alike authorise us to do, or we must continue to give stockholders an unfair advantage, *at the expence and to the certain prejudice of the productive classes*", p. 201. Later McCulloch withdrew this publication from circulation and seems to have regretted what he regarded as an early indiscretion. See Hollander: *Letters of David Ricardo to John Ramsay McCulloch* (American Economic Association), pp. 7–9. But his argument makes very interesting reading in the light of present-day discussions on the burden of fixed interest charges during a period of deflation.

VII

INFLATIONARY ACTION—PUBLIC FINANCE AND BANKING POLICY

I. *Expansion of Credit for Public Finance*

THREE main forms of inflationary action call for notice. The first is the depreciation of the currency, the economic effects of which were considered in Lecture V. The second is the tariff which has been rejected in Lecture III as a useful aid to recovery. Apart from other defects, increases in duties on an already excessive tariff only add to the distortions in the price structure without raising the price level of exports and the national income. This problem will receive further consideration in the concluding lecture. The third form of inflationary action, viz. finance of public expenditure through expansion of credit, is an important and constructive form of inflationary action and calls for detailed examination. It will be remembered that we defined inflationary action as that action which tends to prevent the price level and the national income from falling to a position that would be reached at parity with gold without special effort to increase spending power. The method of finance of Government deficits and loan expenditure through credit expansion is classed as inflationary because it directly maintains a higher level of spending power and national income. The Australian banking and public finance policy in the crisis affords a very interesting illustration of this action. The existence of a deficit in the budget does not, in itself, offer a means for maintaining total spending power in the community. If the deficit is financed from public loans subscribed out of income that would otherwise be spent, the reduction in spending power is the same as the reduction in expenditure or the increase in taxation required for balancing the budget. Usually this would not be the case because even a public loan would provide an avenue for the investment of savings that might otherwise go into hoards during a depression. In the case of Australia, however, the deficits were not financed out of public loans of this nature. The Copland Committee was perhaps not quite alive to the distinction. It urged that borrowing to bridge the gap in the budget was "both justifiable and practicable". It added, however, "this should come from current savings rather than from new bank credits", and suggested also the funding of short-term indebtedness both in Australia and in London as being "necessary to the restoration of Australian credit".[1]

This concession to orthodoxy was perhaps a serious lapse on the part of the Committee, which was doubtless much impressed by the magnitude of the short-term advances made by the banks to the governments. Borrowing for financing deficits or for funding was impracticable at reasonable rates of interest during 1931. Even had it been possible to raise a public loan, the method of expanding central bank credit that was pursued in 1931/32 was a much more satisfactory course of action.

II. *Budget Deficits*

The deficits were greater than those anticipated when the Plan was formulated. Two main reasons may be given in explanation of this failure to realise the objective of the Plan as regards budgets. In the first place, during 1931 and the first half of 1932 the New South Wales Government did not reduce expenditure in conformity with the minimum standards required by the Plan. For example, on business undertakings the reduction of expenditure in 1931/32 on the 1929/30 level was 16% in New South Wales compared

[1] Report, par. 49.

with 28% to 34% in the other States. In the second place, the continued deflation overseas caused the price level of exports to fall, national income continued to fall and this increased budgetary difficulties. The Copland Committee assumed some rise in export prices as a possible means of relief and added, "in the improbable event that at the end of three years overseas prices have not risen it will be necessary then to consider the further steps to be taken to regain complete budgetary and exchange equilibrium. The plan here put forward is one of approach to such equilibrium with caution rather than with precipitation".[1]

At the Conference total deficits of £14·65 m. were contemplated for 1931/32. The deficits realised were £20·8 m. of which New South Wales accounted for £14·2 m. The Commonwealth had a surplus of £1·3 m. In June 1932 the total estimated deficits at the scales of taxation and expenditure then in operation were estimated to be nearly £20 m. As this was greatly in excess of the Plan requirements it was agreed that the Commonwealth should balance its budget for 1932/33, and that the aggregate deficits of the States should be limited to £9 m. The Governments lived up to these expectations, the Commonwealth having, in fact, a surplus of £3·5 m. and the States aggregate deficits of £8·6 m. The Commonwealth surplus, be it noted, was achieved in spite of concessions in taxation amounting to £1 m. and increases in expenditure for relief to farmers of £2·25 m. Moreover, included in the aggregate expenditure of the Governments as a whole is £8 m. for sinking funds. For the current year it would have been possible by continuing the scale of Commonwealth taxation and increasing Commonwealth grants to the States to have balanced the budgets as a whole. This course of action was, however, rejected on the ground that some relief should be given to industry through reductions in taxation, and the States

[1] Report, par. 51.

should be allowed to continue with considerable deficits, pending a recovery in export prices and in national income sufficient to raise their revenues approximately to the level of expenditure reached with possible additional economies.[1] The actual position of the deficits for 1932/33 and those stipulated for 1933/34 is shown in the following table:

BUDGET DEFICITS, 1932/33 AND 1933/34

| | 1932/33 | | 1933/34 |
	Plan	Actual	Agreed at Conference, June 1933
	£,000	£,000	£,000
Commonwealth*	+12	+3,545	—
New South Wales	4,500	4,271	3,950
Victoria	900	856	800
Queensland	1,485	1,554	1,850
South Australia	1,215	1,009	1,100
Western Australia	765	864	750
Tasmania	135	55	50
Total	9,000	8,609	8,500

* Surplus.

III. *The Floating Debt*

Before considering the finance and banking problems involved in this budgetary policy, it will be desirable to set out the position of the floating debt. At the beginning of the crisis Australia raised funds in London by overdraft from a bank and by the issue of treasury bills. At the time

[1] The Commonwealth obtained more benefit from the conversion of the internal debt than the States; it was relieved of war debt payments amounting to nearly £A. 7 m. and it was able to make good its losses on customs and excise by heavy increases in duties and by imposing a sales tax. In these circumstances the economy measures were sufficient even in the difficult year 1931/32 to yield a surplus of £1·3 m. It was doubtless sound policy in 1933/34 to budget for a deficit in the States and to make substantial concessions in Commonwealth taxation. But the ultimate effects of depression policy upon the financial relations of the States and the Commonwealth should be considered by the Loan Council in the near future.

of Sir Otto Niemeyer's visit the total amount of these obligations in London was £18 m. In addition, there was a rapidly growing short-term debt in London to the Commonwealth Bank. After the middle of 1930 it was necessary to reduce the short-term loans obtained in the London money market. This was done by using gold reserves even to the extent, in June 1931, of reducing the legal percentage of gold to notes required to be held by the Commonwealth Bank. By the end of 1931 the floating debt in London, to other than Australian institutions, amounted to less than £5 m., but the total short-term debt itself was £stg. 37·3 m. in London at June 30th, 1932. On that date the internal debt was £A. 45 m. In the year 1932/33 but little real increase in the floating debt took place because the London portion had fallen to £stg. 34 m. while the Australian had increased to nearly £A. 49 m. The details for the several States are shown in the following table:

SHORT-TERM DEBT

	June 30th, 1932		June 30th, 1933	
	London	Australia	London	Australia
	£,000	£,000	£,000	£,000
Commonwealth	10,220	6,330	10,220	3,500
New South Wales	12,675	25,010	10,408	27,890
Victoria	6,697	5,200	6,092	5,570
Queensland	—	—	—	1,115
South Australia	3,816	3,500	3,816	4,520
Western Australia	3,426	4,650	3,098	5,875
Tasmania	491	300	491	405
Total States	27,105	38,660	23,905	45,375
Grand Total	37,325	44,990	34,125	48,875

A further note of explanation in regard to the nature of the floating debt is required. In so far as the debt was created against gold or sterling reserves, it was merely the transfer of assets from these reserves to government securities. The liquidity of the assets was, of course, greatly reduced but the transaction was not, strictly speaking, inflationary. It would not add to spending power. We must note also that it would not decrease spending power in Australia. Had the Government raised an internal loan and used the proceeds to purchase the gold and the sterling reserves, some decline in spending power would have taken place, though it would have been less than the reduction in spending power caused by an equivalent amount of taxation. By drawing upon gold and sterling reserves a reduction in spending power was avoided, but the banks accepted non-liquid government securities in place of the gold and liquid sterling securities formerly held. This is certainly the position with regard to the whole of the external portion of the floating debt. With regard to the internal debt, the position is quite different. To a considerable extent this debt is the result of the underwriting of treasury bills by the Commonwealth Bank. It has, in effect, involved a net expansion of central bank credit. In order to maintain government expenditure and loan works, credit was created by the central bank. This is a familiar road to inflation and there were financial authorities who regarded the whole policy as unsound on the ground that still further depreciation of the currency would follow, with rising prices and the normal consequences of such inflationary action. But there were two important differences between the policy pursued in Australia and that pursued in most countries that have gradually drifted into inflation through unbalanced budgets. In the first place, Australia's policy was carried out in an atmosphere of world deflation, and even in Australia the currency unit was appreciating in terms of goods. The course pursued by Australia was inflationary only in the narrow sense in which we have defined the term. In the second place, expenditure was not increasing as is

150   *Inflationary Action—*

the case normally with inflationary finance. The deficits were, on the whole, declining, and for the year 1932/33 there was no net increase in the total floating debt. It was, indeed, an experiment in controlled inflation, and has every prospect of succeeding.[1]

IV. *The Commonwealth Bank*

What has been the effect on the position of the Commonwealth Bank of these and other financial transactions during the depression? If we take the period June 1928 to June 1932 we shall cover the main forms of inflationary finance undertaken by the Bank. A comparison of the balance sheets at the two dates is given in the table on p. 151, together with the balance sheet for June 1933.[2]

The more important changes from 1928 to 1932 may be summarised as follows:

(a) There was an increase of £7 m. in the note issue and of the assets and liabilities of the note issue department. Notes in the hands of the public were, however, slightly under £25 m. at both dates. The increase in the note issue took the form of an increase of over £7 m. in the notes held by the banks, of which £2·4 m. was added to the notes held

---

[1] The floating debt would have increased had it not been for the issue of public loans bringing in £16 m. in 1932/33 and the normal sales of securities "over the counter".

[2] In some respects the balance sheet for June 1933 presents special features. There is the sterling reserve of £3·9 m. on account of sale of gold, which doubtless accounts for part of the £9 m. short-term London funds in the note issue department. The remainder of this asset and the large increase in "other assets" with consequent reduction of debentures suggests greater liquidity in the reserve against the note issue. It is possible that an increase in exchange funds purchased from the trading banks has been followed by transfer of some of these funds to the note issue department and transfer of some debentures to Australian securities in the banking department. Deposits would rise partly as a consequence of increased exchange purchases, and partly as a result of the conversion loan which gave the Bank temporary funds in London and temporary deposit liabilities to the Government. The reduction of £3·75 m. in the note issue was to the extent of £3·25 m. a reduction of notes held by the banks. This would tend also to increase deposits.

COMMONWEALTH BANK. ASSETS AND LIABILITIES

June	1928	1932	1933
NOTE ISSUE DEPARTMENT			
LIABILITIES	£,000	£,000	£,000
Notes in circulation	44,453	51,303	47,551
Other liabilities	40	43	42
Special reserve premium on gold sold	—	—	3,895
Total	44,493	51,346	51,488
ASSETS			
Gold coin and bullion*	22,486	10,500	11,507
Money at short call in London	—	—	9,000
Debentures and other securities	21,873	40,748	24,023
Other assets	134	98	6,958
Total	44,493	51,346	51,488
BANKING DEPARTMENT			
LIABILITIES			
Capital account	4,000	4,000	4,000
Reserve fund	389	1,407	1,594
Rural credits department	903	2,155	2,254
Deposits	42,488	63,587	74,314
Bills payable, etc.	4,090	3,734	3,714
Total	51,870	74,883	85,876
ASSETS			
Coin and cash balances	1,446	1,029	944
Australian notes	4,351	6,785	6,325
Money at short call in London	9,798	13,267	18,515 †
Short term loans, Australian	3,507	10,687	12,841
British Government securities	15,643	10,501	9,574
Commonwealth securities	735	17,678	26,627
Bills receivable, etc.	3,185	1,858	1,892
Bills discounted, advances, etc.	12,670	12,035	7,979
Bank premises	535	1,043	1,179
Total	51,870	74,883	85,876

* Gold and English sterling in 1933.
† I have included in this item £5·6 m. of funds held temporarily in London on account of conversion loan.

by the Commonwealth Bank.[1] The expansion of the note issue was thus caused by an increase in the bank demand rather than in the public demand for notes.

(*b*) The assets of the note issue department were much less liquid in 1932 than they were at June 1928. The gold reserve had fallen from £22·5 m. to £10·5 m. and the debentures and other securities had increased from £21·9 m. to £40·7 m. At June 1932 a close analysis of the securities shows that the whole were Australian securities, of which £29·6 m. were debentures redeemable in London and £1 m. other securities redeemable in London, making a total of £30·6 m. This, of course, reflects the use of banking and gold reserves by the Governments for meeting external obligations. The position of the Bank had, however, improved in this respect by June 1933, when gold and sterling to the amount of £11·5 m. were held, together with a special sterling reserve of £3·9 m. and other liquid assets.

(*c*) The assets of the banking department show clearly the effects of Government finance. There is a net increase of £23 m. of which short-term loans in Australia account for £7·2 m., and Commonwealth Government securities £17 m. Clearly this is the effect of granting credits to the Governments mainly through the issue of treasury bills.

(*d*) On the liability side the increase of £23 m. is to a large extent explained by the growth of deposits of the trading banks with the Commonwealth Bank. These deposits are not shown in the balance sheet, but an analysis of the balance sheets of the trading banks shows that deposits with the Commonwealth Bank increased from £9·2 m. in June 1929 to £29 m. in June 1932. It is not

[1] The position in June 1933 was a total note issue of £47·5 m., of which the public held £24·2 m. and the banks £23·3 m. The banks had reduced their holdings by over £3 m. and the public by £0·6 m. in the period. The increase in the holdings of the banks during the depression was doubtless due to the transfer of gold from the reserves to the Commonwealth Bank and the tardiness of the banks in accepting deposits with the Commonwealth Bank as a full substitute for their former holdings of gold.

necessary here to trace in detail the effect of treasury bill finance upon banking funds. When the Commonwealth Bank creates credit in the form of treasury bills the effect is to raise total bank deposits by an equivalent amount. Of this, a small part is held as customers' deposits with the Commonwealth Bank and the balance as customers' deposits with the trading banks. Against the latter there is a corresponding asset held by the trading banks in the form of deposits with the Commonwealth Bank which, of course, is the liability undertaken by the Commonwealth Bank against its assets of treasury bills. To some extent the increase in the balances held by the trading banks at the Commonwealth Bank is attributable to the exchange operations of the Commonwealth Bank. It will be remembered that the Bank undertook in December 1931 to purchase exchange from the trading banks and to sell exchange to them as required. Variations in the balances of the trading banks at the Commonwealth Bank would accompany these transactions. It is impossible to state to what extent these balances at June 1932 had been increased on this account. The main increase was undoubtedly caused by treasury bill finance.

A decline in the liquidity of reserves and of external assets and a substantial increase in the internal assets of the banking department are the inevitable results of the methods of finance pursued by the Governments and the Commonwealth Bank during the crisis. If we measure the expansion of credit by the increase of liabilities of the banking department we have an increase of no less than 44 % in the period June 1928 to June 1932. An expansion of credit of this order naturally had a considerable influence upon the supply of funds available to the trading banks, the rate of interest, the spending power of the community and the price level. We shall consider these in order.

V. *The Banking Situation*

First, as to the banking situation. In the early stages of the crisis, when the balance of trade was unfavourable and bank exchange reserves were drawn upon to meet overseas commitments, deposits would tend to decline. There are circumstances in which this might not occur; for instance, if the Government purchased overseas exchange and gave the banks securities. Any form of expansion of credit would indeed avoid the contraction in deposits. If, however, the Government purchased out of current resources, either by taxation or by loan, overseas reserves from the banks, the operation would result in a cancellation of deposits. Bank assets would then be reduced by loss of reserves, and liabilities by loss of deposits. This was happening in 1930 and early in 1931, for deposits of the trading banks fell from £275 m. in March 1930 to £263 m. in March 1931. When opportunities for investment are lacking, loss of deposits is not a serious matter for a bank if there is not an equivalent loss of highly liquid reserves. Unfortunately, it was precisely a loss of this nature that offset the loss of deposits. At the same time the advances of banks were becoming more and more frozen. Banks rather sought to reduce frozen advances. Circumstances thus encouraged a wholly deflationary banking policy. Credit extended to Governments had not in 1930 caused a net expansion of central bank credit of sufficient magnitude to ease the position. This was the period in which gold reserves were exchanged for Commonwealth securities without any net expansion of credit. Thus in June 1930, assets of the banking department of the Commonwealth Bank were still only £51·8 m. compared with £51·9 m. in June 1928. Later, when the issue of treasury bills was made through an expansion of central bank credit, deposits and cash reserves began to increase. The changes in the banking position are shown in the following table:

CASH DEPOSITS AND ADVANCES OF THE TRADING BANKS

Quarter ended	Balances at Commonwealth Bank	Coin and bullion	Australian notes	Total cash	Total deposits	Ratio of cash to deposits	Advances and securities
	£ m.	£ m.	£ m.	£ m.	£ m.	°/₀	£ m.
Sept. 1929	7·5	23·8	12·5	43·8	279·5	15·7	281·9
Dec. 1929	8·4	21·3	13·0	42·5	277·2	15·3	292·0
Mar. 1930	13·5	14·6	14·4	42·3	274·4	15·5	287·7
June 1930	16·9	4·6	16·0	37·4	268·6	13·9	282·0
Sept. 1930	15·7	2·7	17·4	35·7	262·5	13·6	276·7
Dec. 1930	20·8	2·1	16·8	39·8	263·4	15·1	278·0
Mar. 1931	29·7	2·1	17·1	48·9	263·3	18·6	268·9
June 1931	32·2	2·0	18·9	53·2	261·4	20·4	262·6
Sept. 1931	23·0	2·0	20·3	45·2	255·8	17·7	268·4
Dec. 1931	22·2	2·1	18·6	43·0	268·5	16·0	269·8
Mar. 1932	32·1	2·2	18·9	53·2	283·6	18·8	268·2
June 1932	29·1	2·0	18·7	49·8	273·0	18·2	272·9
Sept. 1932	21·9	1·9	17·1	40·9	268·0	15·3	279·4
Dec. 1932	23·2	1·9	16·5	41·6	274·6	15·1	285·8
Mar. 1933	25·6	2·0	16·4	43·9	276·9	15·9	285·0
June 1933	23·6	1·9	15·9	41·3	274·7	15·0	286·9

Four outstanding features of this table demand brief mention. In the first place there is the remarkable change in the cash holdings of the trading banks. Their notes have increased slightly, but in place of gold they now hold balances at the Commonwealth Bank as their principal form of cash reserve. In the second place, the decline in the cash of the trading banks was arrested towards the end of 1930, and coincides with the expansion of central bank credit for governmental purposes. Further, the cash ratio which touched a new low record for Australia also responded, leaving the banks in a much stronger position.[1]

[1] The purchase from the Commonwealth Bank of treasury bills by the trading banks explains the decline in the cash ratio after the middle of 1931.

In the third place, the fall in deposits was arrested in the third quarter of 1931. This also is associated with the increase in central bank credit, but there would naturally be some delay in its effects upon bank deposits. Moreover, the export of gold and the adverse balance of payments would reduce bank reserves proportionately more than deposits. Finally, the decline in advances and securities was checked in the middle of 1931, and total credit outstanding commenced to increase. At the beginning of 1933 it had been restored, despite the fall in prices and national income. In general it may be said that a very unfavourable banking position had developed at the end of 1930, and it has now been greatly improved.

VI. *The Rate of Interest*

With expansion of central bank credit, increasing deposits, no public long-term borrowing and a heavy decline in demand for private investment, the rate of interest naturally fell. But banking policy expedited the fall and pressed the rate below the level it would have reached under a severely deflationary policy. At first the banks offered high rates for deposits, but they found later that the growth of stagnant funds in the form of bank deposits was an embarrassment to them. In the middle of 1931 the three months' deposit rate was still at $4\frac{1}{2}\%$. Higher rates for longer periods up to $5\frac{1}{4}\%$ for two years were in force. By successive steps the rates were reduced, and in July 1933 had reached 2% for 3 months' and 3% for 2 years' deposits. In the bond market the new Australian 4% consolidated stock has shown a steady appreciation since October 1931, when the stock was placed on the market. The effective rate had dropped ·from 5·7% to about 3·7% in July 1933. A less expansionist banking policy and an effort to fund floating debt would have kept up the bond rate. There was indeed much controversy over this aspect of banking and financial policy, and an effort was made by the Commonwealth Bank in October 1932 to commence substantial funding operations when the bonds reached par.[1] It was rightly argued at the time by a minority of bankers and treasurers that this action would have been deflationary. There can be no doubt that a funding operation would have transferred bank deposits

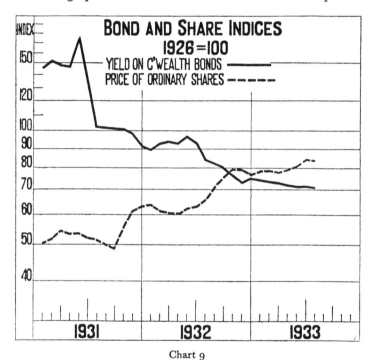

Chart 9

to long-term bonds at 4%, reduced the short-term funds on the money market, and hardened rates of interest generally. Fortunately, the effort was not successful. A loan of £8 m. at $3\frac{3}{4}$% was offered but failed to attract sufficient public support, and a portion was left with the underwriting banks.

[1] A loan of £20 m. at 4% was proposed. £12 m. was to be used for funding purposes and £8 m. for works.

This premature attempt to deal with the floating debt
had the good effect of focusing attention once more upon
the importance of a liberal banking policy in reducing the
rate of interest. Australia had a good opportunity for pur-
suing her policy of expanding central bank credit until she
attained very low interest rates. But the central bank was
gravely concerned about the growth of the floating debt.
When the problem was under consideration in October
1932 the internal floating debt was £52 m., of which
£34 m. was held by the trading banks in the form of
treasury bills discountable at the Commonwealth Bank.
Was there a fear that the trading banks would embarrass
the Commonwealth Bank by presenting their bills for
discount and demanding notes? Or was it merely that the
Bank desired to limit the growth of the floating debt, and
in doing so, to force Governments to even greater efforts
to balance budgets? No doubt pressure of the latter type is
helpful in democracies that might plead any excuse to
follow the line of least resistance. The fear of discounting
was surely groundless. The banks were no doubt glad to
have a satisfactory avenue for the investment of their funds.
They would lose by exchanging treasury bills for notes. Their
cash reserves were sufficient to meet all prospective demands, and there was no evidence of an increase in the
appetite of the public for notes. We must ascribe the Bank's
attitude to the traditional dislike of central banks for a large
floating debt. This type of debt was quite a novelty for
Australia, and the Bank was in any case heavily loaded with
government securities. The real problem, however, was not
so much the magnitude of the debt as the prospect of attaining budget equilibrium and thus ensuring the liquidity
of the bills. To this extent the Bank was on sound ground in
urging caution, but a premature funding of a large block of
the debt would have delayed recovery by maintaining relatively high interest rates. In February 1933 a satisfactory

compromise was reached on the issue. It was tacitly agreed by the Governments and the Bank to finance future public works from public loans, to continue treasury bill finance of deficits, and to proceed with funding operations only if funds were available after the works programme had been met. The rate contemplated was $3\frac{3}{4}\%$, and a £5 m. loan in May at this rate was highly successful.[1] But there is no special virtue in a rate of $3\frac{3}{4}\%$. An era of very low long-term interest rates is necessary for the restoration of investment to a position where current savings can be absorbed. Australia, in common with the rest of the world, suffers at present from too much savings relative to demand for capital. It would be folly to divert these savings into long-term bonds at relatively high rates merely for the purpose of funding a floating debt that is not at present a menace.[2] Australia's task is to stimulate the flow of savings into forms of investment, both public and private, that will involve new spending and employment. A lower rate of interest is the only effective method of achieving this result.[3]

[1] The loan opened on May 22nd and the nominal closing date was June 19th. The Treasurer exercised his option to close the loan at an earlier date by closing it on May 30th, when £8,461,500 had been subscribed.

[2] To fund floating debt is to use savings for expenditure that has already been incurred and financed by expansion of central bank credit. Unless there is some other force increasing spending power and sustaining the price level, the funding operation must contract credit available for other forms of investment. Thus one of the fears of the opponents of public spending, namely, that it diverts credit from private to public investment, is realised. But there is no need for this to happen if the Government is not stampeded into a hasty policy of funding. If funding depresses spending and the price level, the real burden of the public debt is increased. Where, however, a floating debt is increased during a depression as part of a policy designed to maintain prices or check their fall, the increase in the nominal value of the debt might well be less than the increase in the burden of the old debt at the lower price level that would have been reached under a severely deflationary policy. This was certainly the case in Australia, where the old debt was large and would now be an intolerable burden at a much lower price level, despite the reduction in interest.

[3] For my views on Treasury Bill Finance, see Shann and Copland, *The Australian Price Structure*, pp. 109–16.

VII. *Effect on Spending Power*

The future of the floating debt must be considered at the
end of this lecture when we examine the methods by which
the central bank can control banking policy and the money
market with the object of promoting price stability and
reducing the fluctuations in economic prosperity. For the

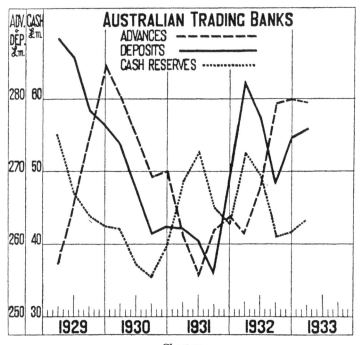

Chart 10

moment, it is sufficient to note that the freedom of the
Commonwealth Bank from some of the restrictions placed
on central banks by recent legislation in other countries has
been a valuable asset to Australia in the crisis. The simple
expedient of a controlled expansion of central bank credit
for public spending has proved to be a more effective
weapon *for expanding credit and increasing spending* than the

more technical method of expansion through purchase of long-term securities; for no central bank has carried the latter method far enough to stimulate spending on a scale that would relieve the depression. I do not suggest that Australia could not have been even less orthodox than the event has proved her to have been. An even greater budget deficit or loan expenditure requiring a greater expansion of central bank credit might theoretically have brought better results. But against this must be placed the important psychological influence of financial opinion as to what is prudent. This raises again the familiar problem of the balance between the inflationary and deflationary types of public action. In the circumstances of early 1931 there was probably no other course open to Australia than one of drastic economy. As already explained in Lecture III, with a less active policy of deflation a higher exchange rate would have been necessary. On the wisdom of contemplating a rise in exchange in April 1931, when the financial crisis was most serious in Australia, the judgment of the Copland Committee quoted above (p. 63) must be regarded as significant. In all the circumstances an expansion of central bank credit of over 40% is no mean record for this depression when the technique of central banking has proved so inept generally in checking the forces of deflation. In Australia, spending power was held up by the issue of treasury bills. Thus the expansion of credit inherent in the growth of the floating debt in its later stages joined with the depreciation of the currency to sustain the domestic price level and to mitigate the impact of world deflation upon the Australian economy.

VIII. *The Price Level*

The success of the policy can be most satisfactorily tested by considering its effect on the price level. But what price level? When we speak of the desirability of raising or sustaining prices we should be specific as to which prices we mean. There are export prices, retail prices, manufacturing prices, wholesale prices in general, and security prices, all of vital concern to the internal economy. Was it sound policy to seek to raise all of these sets of prices? We may answer this question by considering what was the general objective in the recovery plan. In the early stages it was to restore profit in export production and at the same time to "liquify" (as opposed to liquidate) the debt structure. Restoration of investment would follow the fall in interest rates and in real costs arising from successful action on the export industries and the debt structure. This required a closing of the gap between exporters' costs and prices, and a general recovery in security values. Whilst the latter could not be attained under a heavy fall in manufacturing prices, a moderate decline in these prices was not inconsistent with recovery in security values and a general improvement in the liquidity of the debt structure. But a rise in manufacturing prices and in some retail prices, with a consequent widening of the gap between costs and prices in export production, would destroy all prospects of successful action to "liquify" debts. For this reason it was desirable to avoid any increase in manufacturing prices pending a recovery in export prices. Some fall in general prices and in manufacturing prices in particular was desirable if this were accompanied by action to raise export prices. We have seen that the exchange rate was used effectively to maintain export prices at a higher level in Australian currency than would have been possible without the rise in exchange. This was not inconsistent with a fall in manufacturing prices, for the heavy decline in sterling prices of most imports, especially of imports of raw materials, caused import prices even in Australian currency to fall about 20 %. But here, as in other respects, Australian policy was marred by injudicious use of the tariff. Higher duties gave unnecessary shelter to protected goods and the expenditure on loan funds tended to sustain demand at unnecessarily high prices.[1] This need not have happened under a less extreme tariff policy. It was more important to lessen the gap between exporters' prices and costs than to sustain manufacturing prices. As long as prices of exports were depressed by world causes, a considerable disparity between exporters' prices and costs was inevitable. But this disparity was widened by the influence of the tariff in reducing competition from overseas. The expansion of credit for budget deficits and loan works increased the demand for manufactured goods, and thus reduced the unit cost of their production. This credit expansion did not increase the gap between exporters' costs and prices. Had a similar expansion of central bank credit been undertaken by the great industrial countries, Australian export prices would have risen, or would not have fallen so much. In a primary producing country, central bank credit expansion of the type indulged in by Australia can do little to correct distortions in the domestic price structure. It can, however, hold up spending power to some extent, increase the money value of the national income, lower the rate of interest, and assist powerfully in "liquifying" the debt structure. By the end of 1932 share prices had recovered from a low level of 50·4 in September 1931 (base May 1926 as 100) to 81 at the beginning of 1933. This is perhaps a good test of the results of a policy of expansion upon the

[1] Evidence as to the price level of manufactured goods is difficult to obtain. In the wholesale price index number the "industrial group" at the beginning of 1933 showed a rise of 10% on the 1928 level compared with a fall of 32% in the primary products groups. But the "industrial group" is not representative of secondary industry. Mr Howe in *The Case for Protection* publishes a list of price reductions in manufacturing products in the depression. This list suggests average falls from 15% to 20%. Wholesale prices (Melbourne) fell 25% to the beginning of 1933, and retail (Melbourne) 27%. The reduction in manufacturing costs on account of the fall in wages and in prices of raw materials gave considerable scope for price reduction in manufacturing.

general financial situation. At the same time interest on bonds and all other interest rates were falling. Much of this favourable movement took place while the outside world was still suffering from deflation.

Retail prices in Australia moved much more in conformity with wholesale prices than in other countries. This was doubtless a consequence of the heavy fall in prices of food-stuffs. In general, however, the Australian pound was more stable in purchasing power than other currencies. If all price levels are considered in relation to their influence on economic recovery, this is what would be expected to follow from the depreciation of the currency and the addition to spending power made possible by expanding central bank credit. The alteration of the terms of trade, itself a product of the world depression, was the fundamental cause of the disparities in the price structure and the appreciation of the Australian pound in terms of commodities in Australia. With an improvement in the terms of trade, already in process, future policy should aim at maintaining the depreciation of the currency in order to lift export prices. By this means chiefly, and to a less extent by reducing some manufacturing prices and costs that stick, e.g. transport charges, the disparity between exporters' prices and costs will be gradually removed. If an unexpected recovery in export prices to the 1928 level occurs, the whole price level might return to that position. But some financial authorities fear that such a development might cause a rapid expansion of credit on the basis of the great increase in central bank credit that has occurred. If this happened, investment would extend beyond the limits required for recovery. If this credit inflation were accompanied by a resumption of capital imports, internal economic conditions would quickly show the familiar signs of over-investment, and depression would follow. An incipient investment boom seemed a remote contingency in 1932. The rise in export prices and the great recovery in Australian credit abroad, now in process, brings it much closer. Moreover, a depreciated paper currency and an expansion of central bank credit make an excellent seed bed for the growth of an unhealthy boom. Can its growth be checked? If not, it were perhaps better that the seed bed had never been prepared.

IX. *The Future of the Floating Debt*

There are three main grounds upon which the present banking and financial situation is criticised by what might be called "the hard money school".[1]

(*a*) The floating debt is a menace to the Commonwealth Bank in particular, and to the financial structure as a whole.

(*b*) The cash basis of credit has been so enlarged by the issue of treasury bills as to permit a disastrous credit inflation.

(*c*) The currency is insecure under the present exchange mechanism.

With regard to the floating debt, we must distinguish the external from the internal. The former is held almost wholly by the Commonwealth Bank and cannot be reduced without an increase in sterling exchange reserves. A continued favourable balance of payments or a public funding loan in London would raise our sterling reserves and enable some reduction to be made in the external floating debt. If a favourable balance of payments caused exchange funds to accumulate in London, these funds could be used for liquidating floating debt. Australia normally requires a large external banking reserve to meet heavy demands for sterling during an adverse season. This can be steadily built up by transferring external to internal floating debt

---

[1] Radical opinion, overlooking the expansion of credit that has already taken place, and the helpful control of exchange by the banking system, ignores these criticisms, and demands still more credit expansion at all costs. Space does not permit of an examination of this point of view I am concerned here with the means whereby we can preserve what is good in the banking policy during the crisis.

and increasing the sterling assets of the Commonwealth Bank. No prospective increase in London funds from a favourable balance of payments need in these circumstances be urged as a reason for appreciating the Australian pound in terms of sterling. A funding loan might, however, improve our sterling assets so rapidly as to encourage the Commonwealth Bank to bring the exchange rate nearer parity.[1] This would be short-sighted policy. Temporary financial strength is an inadequate basis for a permanent change in economic policy, for an appreciation of the currency would damp down recovery by depressing the price level and by widening once more the gap between exporters' prices and costs. A reduction in the external floating debt is desirable, but it would be unwise to make it a basis for appreciating the currency. By encouraging recovery and an expansion of export and protected production, the present depreciation of the currency is an effective instrument for liquidating the external floating debt over a period.

The internal portion of the debt raises different problems. It would be increased by the suggested method of reducing the external portion.[2] If so, the internal floating debt, it might be argued, is an even greater menace. What is this menace? The banks might present their bills to the Commonwealth Bank and demand notes.[3] They would thus ex-

[1] For reasons to be given in the last lecture, any tendency to resume long-term lending is to be discouraged. A funding loan would be a signal for its resumption.

[2] This is not necessary in all circumstances. If conditions were highly favourable in Australia and the balance of payments were showing a large surplus on current account, a public internal loan could be used to liquidate short-term external securities held by the Commonwealth Bank. This is one method of control open to the Government and the Bank.

[3] The present banking law requires the resumption of the 25% legal reserve (gold or sterling) against notes on July 1st, 1935. The limit of the increased demand for notes would be £40 m. if banks presented all their bills for re-discount. This would necessitate a reserve of £22 m. against a note issue of about £88 m. The present reserve appears to be £20 m. But this view of the menace of the floating debt is surely academic!

change a profitable asset for a dead one. This surely is not a tenable thesis. There is another possible ground upon which the trading banks might seek to re-discount a portion of their bills. This is considered below. If the banks showed an illogical unwillingness to hold treasury bills, the difficulty could be overcome by widening the market for the bills. At present the market is limited to the banks, and there are demands for the bills by other financial institutions.[1] The short-term money market in Australia can in fact carry with advantage a quantity of treasury bills that is at present indeterminate. Until the market is tested, it is absurd to speak of the internal floating debt being a menace merely because it is unfamiliar. As a legacy from the crisis it might well offer a permanent and much-prized avenue for investment of short-term funds. The persistence of unbalanced budgets, involving an expansion of the debt, is a real menace. Treasury bills are then an uncertain asset. Given budget equilibrium, there is no reason to suppose that the Australian money market cannot profitably absorb treasury bills. The amount must be ascertained by experiment in more settled conditions, when the market for the bills has been extended and the Commonwealth Bank has improved its technique by quoting a variable rate of re-discount.

X. *Control of Banking and Currency*

A wider market for the bills and a variable rate of re-discount would act as checks upon the trading banks in their use of the bills as a basis for credit inflation.[2] If these checks were insufficient, there are two other powerful weapons available to the Government and the Bank in controlling

---

[1] In these circumstances, it is somewhat inconsistent to suggest that the banks might seek to re-discount their bills and embarrass the Commonwealth Bank.

[2] If prices rose rapidly under credit inflation, the public demand for notes might increase and banks might then desire to re-discount some bills. But this demand could be met without embarrassing the Commonwealth Bank. Far more important would be the economic consequences of credit inflation.

the situation. A funding loan could be issued. This would harden interest rates, reduce the volume of bills, and reduce bank deposits.[1] Alternatively, the Bank, with its freedom to manage the currency in the interests of the community at large, could vary its rates for purchasing and selling London funds. By appreciating the Australian pound in the conditions assumed, the Bank would check the internal demand for credit, increase the demand for sterling funds, and reduce the cash resources of the banks. In Australian conditions this is an important form of central bank control. In normal times, wide variations in the Bank's purchasing and selling rate for exchange need not be contemplated, though considerable latitude might be a remote necessity in present circumstances. This suggests that a permanent feature of Australian exchange control should be a sterling exchange standard, with rates fixed by the central bank within limits considerably wider than the old gold points.

But the Bank may exercise still two other forms of control. There is the consultation with the trading banks as to the general nature of banking policy appropriate to changing economic conditions. The Bank's relations with the trading banks are cordial, and a tradition of consultation is rapidly being established. The power of personal persuasion is more effective than acts of coercion, and the banking system of Australia has shown much evidence in recent years of the beneficial results of conference. There is no evidence of a determined effort on the part of the trading banks to embark upon action that is embarrassing to the Commonwealth Bank and also contrary to sound banking practice. If, however, conference failed, the Bank could add to its other forms of control the purchase and sale of government securities of which it holds a large amount. I need not dis-

[1] A funding loan is a last step, for we do not yet know the volume of the bills that the money market can profitably absorb. The other forms of control would probably be adequate pending recovery from the depression.

cuss here the familiar problem of open market operations, but it is important to note that the market for government securities in Australia is limited. The Bank would find this form of control less effective than either variable rates for purchase and sale of London funds or a wider bill market with variable re-discount rates.

With these forms of control at its disposal, the Bank, supported by the Government, as it is on present official policy, need not fear unhealthy credit expansion on the basis of the present internal floating debt. Consider finally the alleged insecurity of the Australian currency under present conditions. In Lecture V, I suggested the development of a sterling exchange standard as an ultimate objective of monetary policy. There is in fact such a standard in operation at present, but legally the Bank is not compelled to give sterling in exchange for Australian currency. In practice it does, though it reserves to itself the right to vary the rate at which it will make this exchange. In refusing to tie the currency to sterling or any other standard at present, the Bank is adding to rather than detracting from the security of Australian currency, for it is endeavouring to preserve a currency unit less variable in internal purchasing power than other and more important currencies. This is a constructive exchange policy. By promoting export production and thus adding to sterling assets, it improves the security of the currency. In changing world conditions, internal stability is preferable to exchange stability, whatever be the inconveniences of variations in the rate of exchange.[1] With more settled conditions overseas and a return to profitable enterprise in export production, Australia may once again stabilise her currency in terms of an international system. Her present freedom of action is a

[1] The events of the crisis have served to confirm this view, which I expressed in 1924, before the return to gold, in the Presidential Address to Section G of the Australasian Association for the Advancement of Science.

guarantee that she will not be prematurely tied to sterling or any other international system. An improving budgetary situation and increasing sterling reserves are the real forces determining the security of the currency. Stability with a fluctuating international standard may cause unnecessary economic distress in Australia. Ideas of a "natural" rate of exchange have little application to present conditions when the world has suffered from the most unnatural monetary phenomena ever witnessed. In any case the so-called natural rate rarely operated in Australia, for large variations in London funds took place without frequent changes in the rate. Until it is safe to link the currency again with the international standard, control can be exercised by the Commonwealth Bank to maintain any rate that promotes recovery and ultimate price stability in Australia, whatever be the temporary accumulation of London funds. Australian currency is in fact at present more stable than most other currencies, and therefore more secure.

VIII

FORMS OF CONTROL FOR ECONOMIC RECOVERY

I. *Australia and World Economic Conditions*

"AUSTRALIA is leading the way bravely in the great endeavour to bring the labouring population as a whole up to a high level of cultural and physical equipment."[1] In these words Marshall summed up the traditional economic policy of Australia. The brave endeavour was made, as we have shown, in favourable circumstances during the first thirty years of the present century. But there were unmistakable signs at the end of the period that the effort was sustained only by forcing developmental policy beyond sound economic limits. Then came the great depression with its exposure once more of the weakness of an economy that relied too much on external aids—high export prices and external borrowing.

A high standard of living could be maintained while resources were high relative to population, the terms of trade favourable and the inrush of overseas capital heavy. Even these conditions could not sustain the standard of living with a rapidly increasing population. The rate of increase was declining before 1930 and unemployment was increasing. The depression accelerated these movements and confirmed the view of an increasing number of observers that a change of economic policy was inevitable. In Lecture I, I have indicated the steps that were taken from 1926 to 1929 to prepare for the inevitable change. After 1929 attention was focused on measures necessary to meet the immediate difficulties created by the financial and economic

[1] Marshall, *Industry and Trade*, p. 160.

crisis. How far have these measures laid the foundation of a permanent change in economic policy? That is the main question to which we must address ourselves in this final lecture.

It is impossible to give a complete answer in the compass of a single lecture, and it may yet be too early to evaluate correctly the permanent effects of the crisis measures. Moreover, the impact of external social and economic policy upon the Australian economy is still unspent. What is to be the future of international trade in raw materials, metals and food-stuffs? What will be the direction of the flow of international investment in the next era of world economic development? What permanent monetary changes will result from the efforts of many countries to manage their currencies? What fundamental changes in economic control will follow from the political and social revolutions at present proceeding in America and Europe? What will be the economic effect of the rapid industrialisation in the East? These questions cannot be answered in a world of transition, but the problems they raise must be noted in evaluating the permanent effects upon Australia of the economic policy she has pursued in the past three years.

To make discussion intelligible it is perhaps necessary to commence with certain assumptions concerning the effects of world economic movements upon Australia. It would be rash to prophesy at this moment of revolutionary change in world economic affairs. My assumptions are therefore not to be construed as forecasts.

They are as follows:

(*a*) That the standard of living of European and Far Eastern peoples will be raised by the economic development that follows the passing of the depression.

(*b*) That international investment will be lower in volume and less concentrated upon countries producing raw materials and food-stuffs.

(*c*) That economic control in the form of regulating industrial conditions, imports and monetary systems will be intensified in Europe and America.

(*d*) That demand for raw materials and food-stuffs from the Far East will be sustained and even increased.

By no means are all of these assumptions unfavourable to Australia. Increasing control of production and imports in the outside world will hamper the flow of international trade in Australian exports but the higher standard of living will be a compensating influence. With the exception of wheat, the demand for Australian exports is elastic and will respond to improved world conditions. Wheat is perhaps the one export that is definitely over-produced at the moment, and the return to normal conditions in the wheat trade may be somewhat delayed. But on all except her marginal lands Australia can produce wheat at surprisingly low costs. Though capital losses may be severe in her wheat areas she can sustain her output with perhaps the abandonment of some marginal lands.[1] Her greatest industry, wool, is assured of a permanent demand, though less favourable seasons may increase costs and retard recovery. Even in wheat and to some extent in dairy products the present low export prices are in part caused by the tariff and fiscal policy of importing countries at present under the spell of economic nationalism. With the progress of economic recovery and the revival of secondary industry in these countries the barriers against imports of food-stuffs and raw materials will doubtless be relaxed. Some fall in prices

---

[1] In 1930 Professor Wadham estimated wheat costs in marginal Victorian land with 11 bushels per acre as a reasonable expectation at 4*s*. 6*d*. per bushel at country stations. With costs down by 25% the payable price would be 3*s*. 2*d*. at country stations, or about 3*s*. 8*d*. at Melbourne. With currency depreciated nearly 50% on gold this is not likely to be greatly in excess of ruling prices. As many farmers in the districts concerned are financially dependent upon the Government, they will doubtless be assisted rather than driven off the land. But the average yield on all marginal land is not 11 bushels per acre.

in importing countries and some rise in prices in exporting countries will follow. This indeed is one of the fundamental adjustments in the world price structure that must accompany economic recovery.

Australia will profit by this movement. Her terms of trade should, on the whole, improve. As the supply of her exports is normally inelastic, recent increases in their volume are in part a consequence of the national effort to sustain income in the great export industries. With a recovery in price this effort will doubtless be relaxed, and seasonal conditions will not be so propitious. But a unit of exports will purchase more imports and sustain a higher national income. We cannot, however, expect a steady expansion of export production at favourable prices, nor can we expect a resumption of the flow of international investment in Australia at the old level. While, therefore, there are reasons for assuming that Australia may, on the whole, sustain the present volume of export production at more favourable prices, there is little basis for the all too common assumption that Australia's resources will permit of a resumption of development at the old rate. All recent geographical research in Australia emphasises the limitation of resources and their rigid control by climate.[1] Moreover, we are living

---

[1] An excellent short account of the conditions in Australian export industries is given in the chapters contributed by Professor S. M. Wadham to Copland (Editor), *An Economic Survey of Australia* (Annals of American Academy of Political and Social Science, Nov. 1931). See also in the same publication Associate Professor Wood's discussion of physical and climatic factors controlling settlement and population growth. Conditions of production in export industries as a whole, and the improvement in prices of primary products relative to secondary usually associated with recovery from acute depression, justify the conclusion that income from export production will rise from the low levels of 1931 and 1932; but a higher export income is necessary to consolidate recent expansions of export production, and to adjust the debt structure in primary production. Whilst the rise in export income will offer scope for some increase in employment it will not serve as a basis for absorbing population increasing at a rate of $1\frac{1}{2}\%$ to 2% per annum. We must expect a much lower rate of growth with immigration at a nominal figure and natural increase at little more than half the old rate of 1·5% per annum. For 1932 the natural increase was only 0·83% compared with

in the twentieth century with its emphasis upon the
amenities of life that make for a higher standard of living
of populations that increase but slowly. Australia has less
of these amenities to offer to world trade than of basic
needs. In the Victorian era it was international traffic in
the food-stuffs that opened up new lands overseas and promoted increasing investment in these lands.

Australia, in common with other great overseas producers of food-stuffs, cannot hope to resume the march of
her economic development at the old pace. This would be
true even if she were splendidly endowed by nature. A
slackening of pace with a much reduced inflow of both
capital and people appears inevitable in the new world
economic forces that are now emerging from the depression. To some extent Australia will profit by industrialisation in the East, where she has already established a
flourishing export trade for nearly all her products. She
must continue to look towards the East for light—Empire
agreements cannot offer the outlet she urgently needs for
food-stuffs that are now produced in increasing quantities
by Great Britain herself.

II. *Investment and the Problem of Control*

This then is the economic background in which Australia
must make her final effort towards complete economic recovery. She has one advantage over most other countries.
Long before the economic crisis Australia had served an
apprenticeship in economic regulation. She made many
mistakes and has now some appreciation of the cost of an
ambitious policy of development in a closely regulated
economy. As Marshall himself remarked: "It appears in-

1·25% for the period 1921–32. The corrective to economic pressure on the
standard of living is a lower rate of population growth, and Australia will no
doubt pursue this course. But for some years the high post-war birth rate
will furnish industry with an unusually large number of workers seeking
employment. This is a problem not peculiar to Australia.

deed that her procedure involves certain forms of restriction which might prove fatal to a country whose natural resources are on a less generous scale than hers". To one who has lived through the later years of Australia's policy of economic control there is something tragic in the universal enthusiasm now shown by the Northern Hemisphere for measures of economic control frequently of a restrictive nature.[1] In the heyday of our socialistic experiments in Australia we were fit subjects for academic study. But men of affairs in the old world with our example before their eyes, and that of our sister Dominion across the Tasman Sea, now warmly embrace economic doctrines which Australia after thirty years' experience has found in some respects unsatisfactory.[2] Apart from excesses in tariff policy, which we now struggle to correct, the economic policy we pursued in the crisis was designed to encourage private enterprise. New measures of control were confined largely to management of the currency to give private industry a monetary unit reasonably stable in purchasing power. It is no exaggeration to say that this remains, even in Australia, and much more so in the world at large, the most important immediate economic problem. To ensure a balance between costs and prices in industry, Australia used her existing machinery of industrial regulation and budgetary control to reduce costs. To some extent she

[1] British policy was justly described recently by a speaker at the Trade Union Congress as "price raising through scarcity".

[2] For an account of the results of State enterprise see Eggleston, *State Socialism in Victoria* (King). By far the most vigorous attack yet launched against the banking structure in Australia is now in progress. Nationalisation of banking is demanded and may well become the war cry at the next Commonwealth elections. Whatever may be said of banking policy in the past, the Australian banks as a whole have pursued a far more enlightened policy in this depression than the banks of most other countries. Yet it is mainly in respect of their recent policy that they are criticised to-day. Great Britain adopted a tariff after depreciating her currency when any case for the tariff was undermined by the change in monetary policy. Surely Australia will not follow her example by changing a vital element of economic policy at a time when events have proved the efficiency of the existing institutions administering that policy.

relaxed her restrictions on industry[1] while concentrating upon monetary and budget control as her main form of collective effort. In a crisis when values are collapsing rigid adherence to a gold standard is the most restrictive of all forms of regulation. Had Australia attempted her adjustment on a gold basis she would be to-day in the precarious position of some European countries that profess to maintain parity with gold.

The old world will doubtless witness many experiments in control of production, regulation of labour conditions, forced economic development and state enterprise. As in Australia some of these experiments will succeed, but many will fail and involve heavy economic loss. Australia passed through this phase of her development in more propitious times, and she has now to bear some of the costs. But unless there is a violent political upheaval her economy will not be upset in the immediate future by further steps along a well-worn and somewhat discredited path.[2] Her task is to provide the background in which private enterprise may develop sufficiently to absorb the present unemployed and the new supplies of labour from a population *that will increase at a much lower rate than formerly.* The benefits of the lower rate of population growth in sustaining the standard of living will not at first be apparent. For, as indicated above (p. 174, n.), the high post-war birth rate has temporarily increased the proportion of the population in the age group 15 to 24. This makes the problem of population absorption difficult at the moment. But it is a passing phase and the present population trend is unmistakable. Thus in

---

[1] The suspension of rural awards of wages and working conditions in Queensland and New South Wales is the most striking illustration.

[2] I do not suggest that the movement towards increasing "corporative control" in joint stock enterprise and the regulation of public utilities that had produced great change in capitalism in this century are not wholly desirable. It is the gospel of widespread state ownership and regulation, or more correctly interference, that seems in the light of Australian experience open to challenge.

a recent review of population trend in Australia Mr H. J. Exley remarks: "The natural increase experienced has decreased progressively until the rate for 1931 is less than half that for 1891. The birth rate has recently fallen to a very low level in Australia (18·2 for 1931), thus approaching closely the rate just sufficient to maintain a stable population at 1921 mortality rates. In the last three years there has been a net loss of over 28,000 by migration. The continuation of such movements cannot but have a serious effect on our future growth, and only hastens the time when a stationary population will eventuate".[1]

The problem of control in Australia is not to force the rate of growth of population by immigration as in the past, but to encourage private enterprise to expand national income sufficiently to absorb a lower rate of growth of population at a rising standard of living. In the past we went too far along the wrong road in economic control. By a direct attack upon development, wages and working conditions we sought to maintain a high standard of living for a population that was growing much more rapidly than is commonly supposed. We did nothing to control the flow of investment at a reasonable rate of interest or to ensure reasonable stability in the price level. Consumers' income was maintained at the expense of increasing costs—real wages, the real rate of interest, the real burden of taxation. Perhaps the United States is treading the same path at present. Time alone will tell. We do know that the experiment failed in Australia to reach its objective, partly because it was forced too much along wrong lines, and partly because it neglected some vital elements of economic control. The evils of a varying price level are now widely understood, and public policy that aims at promoting stability of prices, after economic equilibrium has again been reached, will be widely supported. I have sketched the lines of such a policy

[1] *The Economic Record*, June 1933, p. 94.

in the preceding lecture. This must be a cardinal feature of control in the future. But it must be associated with efforts to promote a regular flow of investment. In some respects this is a matter of keeping down the burden of total interest payments on lines that are advocated later in this lecture. Something can be done also by varying the flow of public investment. This is a matter for the Loan Council and the banking system. The use of the treasury bill will avoid disturbances to the money market if the Government decides to increase its loan expenditure during adverse economic conditions, and to keep it below the average amount in better times. But the problem is not one merely of maintaining a regular flow of investment. There must also be a sufficient flow of investment to absorb savings in new construction works. The alternative for Australia, not for the world as a whole, is to increase export and protected production by an amount equal to the difference between domestic savings on the one hand and home investment minus external borrowing on the other. The same result could be attained by a fall in the standard of living. The first adjustment does not seem practicable, while the second is neither practicable nor desirable. The real solution is a rate of interest sufficiently low to encourage the necessary volume of investment. Something can be done in this direction by banking policy, especially in preventing the rate from rising too high when investment is active. But this is a matter more of regulating changes in the rate than of ensuring a permanently lower rate. There are two difficulties in the way. First, Australia is a member of a world economy and her real rate of interest cannot for long depart seriously from the real external rate. In the second place, much Australian lending is for long-term agricultural and pastoral loans where the risks of variations in output are considerable. In the future, with the development of intensive farming, especially pasture improvement, in the areas of more settled weather, this risk element may be reduced. The rate will, however, remain relatively high and is likely to prevent investment proceeding at a sufficient pace to ensure the full use of savings in industry. Allowance must be made for this contingency in considering the extent to which economic recovery is possible in existing circumstances and with such modifications in policy as seem practicable. We now proceed to examine this problem.

III. *The Conditions of Recovery*

We may recall the division of Australian income into export, sheltered and protected income. For 1926/27 the Committee on the Tariff estimated export income and protected income each at about 25 % of the total income, and sheltered at one-half.[1] In the depressed conditions of 1930/31 the proportion of protected income, including protected primary production as in the former estimate, increased at the expense of export income.[2] This result was caused almost wholly by the distortion in the price structure during the depression. Volume of production for export income increased while volume for protected income, despite the increase in volume in protected primary production (butter, sugar, fruit), declined. The higher relative prices for secondary products, partly an inevitable result of the depression and partly a consequence of the heavy increases in the tariff, sustained the value of protected income. Export income was exposed to the full blast of world depression. Sheltered income is largely a passive element in national income. It consists of those goods and services that by their nature are not open to world competition. Its value is

---

[1] *The Australian Tariff: An Economic Inquiry.*

[2] Estimated on the same basis as in 1926/27 the figures for 1930/31 were as follows:

			£
Export income	...	...	80 m.
Protected income	...	...	110 m.
Sheltered income	...	...	240 m.

ultimately dependent upon the value of export and protected income; its volume upon the ratio of its price level to that of the other two elements of national income. As in protected income there is a resistance of sheltered income to price adjustment in a depression. If prices of export income are very low the price level of protected and sheltered income can be sustained only at the expense of volume. Hence in sheltered and protected income a large volume of unemployment must arise, unless the ratio of exchange between export income on the one hand and protected and sheltered income on the other is restored to its equilibrium level. That is the main problem of economic adjustment as already indicated.

For complete recovery and absorption of unemployed in Australia an additional change has to be made in the whole economy. The ratio of internal costs to external costs generally must be lowered. This is required in Australia for two reasons—the less favourable terms of trade and the reduced inflow of capital. From both these changes in the economy there is a fall in real income which can be made good only by increasing export or protected income. Both these elements can be expanded by increasing efficiency relative to efficiency of external producers. In export income the problem is to secure an increasing share of world demand for export products. In protected income the problem is to secure an increasing share of the domestic market for import products, without adding to the cost of these products to domestic consumers. If protected income expands through an increase in the production of protected goods at prices substantially above the duty free price of imports there may be a net loss of national income. For the higher price of protected goods supplanting imports will add ultimately to the cost of living, and to all costs in industry, thus reducing real wages and real incomes, especially in export production. If, however, the output of protected products is increased at the duty free price of imports, there is a net addition to national income with results just as beneficial as if export production at world prices had been expanded to add a similar value to export income.

The problem of expanding national income to its former real level must therefore be one of increasing export and protected income to compensate for the loss of real income caused by reduced overseas borrowing, and the less favourable terms of international trade. The increase in export and protected income would then sustain sheltered income at its old real level. It is possible to estimate the magnitude of the task required for making up the loss of income in this way. We must, however, make certain assumptions:

(*a*) Let the terms of international trade have moved against Australia since 1928 by 12·5%. This means that, on the basis of 1928, export prices would be 70 and import prices 80, both in Australian currency.

(*b*) Let the expansion of export production be on the average 15% above the pre-depression level. For 1932/33 it was over 30%, but we must make allowance for a very favourable season.

(*c*) Let the reduction of external borrowing be from £30 m. to £10 m. (sterling) at the 1928 price level. This presupposes an average annual inflow of capital of less than £stg. 8 m. at present prices, or approximately £A. 10 m. There is a real reduction of two-thirds.

(*d*) Let the fall in Australian external interest payments be of the order of £stg. 5 m. from £stg. 33 m. since 1928.

(*e*) Finally, let the improved efficiency in protected income be such as to have laid the foundation for an expansion of 5%.

In view of the reduction in costs in all industries and the efforts to improve efficiency, these assumptions are on the whole reasonable. The third is perhaps open to serious question, but we are concerned here with assumptions in keeping with what is likely to happen and not with what ought to happen. The overseas investor will no doubt shortly be looking to Australia, as to other new countries, for opportunities of investment. We have already experienced some flow of capital from abroad into the gold-mining industry and some protected industries, and sooner or later some new public loans will doubtless be sought.

The problem confronting Australia is to restore employment at least to its pre-depression level. For reasons given in the first lecture there was abnormal unemployment then. Reconstruction should ultimately proceed far enough to eliminate this unemployment. Employment is available from production in export, protected and sheltered industries. But since production in sheltered industries is dependent upon export and protected production it will suffice to concentrate upon changes in export and protected industries. Any change in these industries ultimately affects imports. A decrease in export prices, and in the total value of exports, promotes finally a fall in imports. An increase in protected production may offset the fall in exports, so that a change in imports may not signify any change in national income and demand for labour. If export production declines, or the price level of exports falls more than the price level of imports, and no change takes place in protected production, there must be a fall in real national income and in the demand for employment. For in this case the real costs of imports rise, and this causes a rise in real costs of production generally. If the same amount of imports is required for maintaining production and the standard of living, that is, if protected production does not expand to compensate for the altered terms of trade, more goods must be exported to purchase the former quantity of imports. If exports can be expanded sufficiently to purchase the old volume of imports there will be no loss of real income. Similarly, an expansion of protected production supplies the country with goods formerly imported, and a corresponding reduction in imports is then possible without loss of real income. By measuring changes in the volumes of export and protected production and of imports, we can present in a fairly simple and concrete form the changes required in the internal economy to restore real income to its pre-depression level. If the fall in volume of imports that can be purchased at the given value of exports is offset by expansion of protected production there is no loss of real income. Improved efficiency has in this case offset the higher relative costs of imports without any fall in the standard of living. The deficiency in the volume of imports below the old volume minus the increased volume of protected production is an indication of the loss of real income. Imports are not to be regarded as income if we are considering income as the source of demand for employment. In this sense income is made up of output in export, protected and sheltered production. But inability to purchase the old volume of imports unaccompanied by no expansion, or an insufficient expansion of protected production, signifies a loss of income.

Let x and x' be respectively the old and new volumes of imports. Then

$$x - x' = \text{loss of real income from exports } (y)$$
$$- \text{increase in protected production } (z).$$

If $y = z$, there is no loss of real income, and this will occur as export production expands, export prices rise and protected production expands. We can, therefore, profitably consider the effects of changes in export and protected production upon the volume of imports as a means of measuring loss of income.

Before the depression our imports were of the order of £140 m. This is lower than the level of imports on the average of the years 1923 to 1929 given in Lecture V, but I have taken the base for export and import prices as 1928. This, together with the assumption of only £5 m. reduction in overseas interest, compensates for any tendency to take a lower figure for imports and for exports. With a fall in import prices in Australian currency of 20 % the same volume can be purchased to-day for £A. 112 m. Taking £140 m. as the value of exports before the depression, the fall of 30 % in the value of exports and the rise of 15 % in volume gives an export of £A. 113 m., but borrowing is assumed to be only £stg. 8 m. and interest payments to be £stg. 28 m. leaving a balance of £stg. 20 m. or £A. 25 m. to be met. Imports can therefore be not £A. 113 m. but only £A. 88 m.[1] The loss is thus of the order of £A. 24 m. (£A. 112 m. – £A. 88 m.). But we have assumed that protected income has increased by 5 %. Before the depression protected income was about £150 m., which at present prices would be about £120 m. This latter figure is obtained by assuming a 20 % drop in prices in protected income as in imports. An expansion of 5 % adds £A. 6 m. by which imports can fall without any loss of income. Thus the new level of imports would be £A. 106 m. and not £A. 112 m. The real reduction of imports would be £A. 18 m. (£A. 106 m. – £A. 88 m.) and not £A. 24 m. To make good this loss export and protected income would have to be expanded by this amount, that is by 10 % in the aggregate from the position assumed. If this expansion took place there would be no loss of real income in Australia and no case for postulating a reduction in the standard of living.

IV. *Tariff Costs and National Income*

If the conditions assumed had all been in operation in 1931/32 and 1932/33 we may suppose that the progress of economic recovery would have been much more marked than has been noticeable in these two years. In these years

[1] At this figure imports plus interest payments balance exports at £A. 113 m.

the terms of trade were much less favourable than we have assumed, overseas borrowing negligible and the volume of protected income much contracted. In addition internal investment was greatly reduced, and this contracted both protected and sheltered income. We may suppose that internal investment will expand with recovery to a level equal to the present real value of annual capital raised internally before the depression plus the very greatly reduced external borrowing we have assumed.[1] The terms of international trade, with export prices down 30 % and import prices down 20 % on 1928, are not less favourable to Australia than those actually in operation in the current export season. But the full effects of the recent rise in export prices on the national economy will not be felt even during the present export season. It is our assumption concerning protected income that perhaps raises most difficulties. It is true that some protected industries have acquired an increasing share of the domestic market at lower prices than those prevailing before the depression. But the decline in overseas borrowing and in investment generally has caused a heavy contraction of other elements of protected income and of sheltered income. Moreover, the present volume of protected income is a greater relative burden on export production than was the 1926/27 volume which the Tariff Committee of 1929 found to have added 9 % to costs in export income. On the same method I have estimated the added costs of protection for 1930/31 at 16 %

[1] New investment for public works will not fall by the amount of the decline in external borrowing. At existing costs £32 m. of investment has the same real value as £40 m. before the depression. Perhaps £20 m. will in future be the value of public investment. If so, the decline will be £4 m. less than the present value of the decline in external borrowing supposed. Private investment can decline by a similar amount and leave investment at the level assumed. In the altered circumstances a decline in the real level of private investment of much more than £4 m. would be expected, but we have to include in private investment some things formerly done by the State, an expansion of export income of the order assumed, and some expansion of protected income.

to 18% on export income. With the rise in export prices and the consequent increase in export income this figure will now be smaller, but it remains higher than before the depression and is a barrier to the expansion of export income so necessary for complete recovery in the new post-crisis conditions. Expansion of protected income at this cost is not a method of increasing real national income, but rather of sustaining money income while decreasing real income.

Reports of the Tariff Board in the past two years have emphasised the danger of the excessive protection built up during the depression. The Board, as will be indicated later, has greatly improved its technique of testing the economic value of an industry, and the degree to which tariffs should be applied. It is in an unrivalled position to estimate the effects of protection and has for some time been engaged in reviewing the effects of the high duties imposed in the tariff changes of 1930. In the Annual Report for 1931/32 the Board gave many illustrations of excess costs and referred to the tariff in relation to employment in strong terms: "The imposition of high rates of duty for the benefit of one industry, resulting in seriously higher costs to other secondary or to primary industries, may cause some additional employment in the one, but resultant unemployment in the others. The maximum employment of our people is largely dependent upon the successful expansion of our export industries. This expansion, though largely affected by the world's demand for our products, is also bound up with low costs of production. The establishment of new industries or the extension of existing industries which need the application of excessive rates of duty tends to add to costs and retard progress and employment".[1]

[1] Quoted in Shann and Copland, *The Australian Price Structure*, 1932, p. 224. The comparison of tariff costs to-day and in 1926/27, when the original investigation was made, is fraught with difficulties because of exchange, the much higher level of duties and the increasing competition of overseas pro-

V. *Depression Policy and the Future*

This digression on the tariff and the position of protected income was necessary to emphasise the effects of high tariffs in hindering the recovery of real income. It exposes a possible source of optimism in our original assumptions and indicates that the loss of income still to be made good is perhaps of the order of £A. 24 m. and not £A. 18 m. But this is the loss still to be met to restore the real income available before the depression, and the standard of living then in operation. If the standard of living falls by 10%, as the economists argued during the crisis was necessary, the problem is quite different. We then require a real income 10% below the pre-crisis level. In other words we can afford in these circumstances, and on all the assumptions made above, to allow imports to fall to approximately £A. 96 m. This leaves an expansion of export and protected income of only £A. 8 m. to make good the final loss. So satisfactory a result is, however, dependent upon not only the somewhat reasonable assumptions made regarding the terms of trade and the expansion of export production, but also upon the less satisfactory assumptions concerning the

ducers to enter the Australian market at reduced prices. In addition there were prohibitions and rationing of imports in 1930/31. In recent tariff controversies in Australia protectionists have claimed that the depreciation of the currency is responsible for a large part of the difference between the prices of manufactured products in Australia and abroad and the consequent excess costs of protected production (see Howe, *The Case for Protection*, published by the Chamber of Manufactures, N.S.W. 1933, pp. 46–8). This claim ignores (*a*) the heavy fall in costs in Australian industry even in terms of the depreciated currency, (*b*) the effect of currency depreciation upon income in export industries, and (*c*) the fall in the prices of imports. Even in terms of depreciated currency, with lower wages and generally lower prices for raw materials, costs of protected industries have not been raised by the depreciation of the currency. Export income has benefited by the higher prices received in local currency. Any appreciation of the currency would it is true expose protected producers to increasing competition from overseas with a corresponding reduction in costs. By reducing the cost of landing goods duty free this appreciation would widen the margin between Australian prices of protected goods and import prices, thus increasing the relative costs of protected goods. At the same time the prices of export products would fall rendering export producers less able to bear the excess costs of protection.

import of capital and the expansion of protected income. Moreover, internal investment must be expanded to the limits suggested above. In these conditions the conclusion is inescapable that for the present the reduction in the standard of living is inevitable. With real incomes down by 10 % on the average, the required value of sheltered income can be sustained on a real value of export and protected income 10 % less than their combined former value plus the real loss in borrowing.[1] We arrive therefore at the conclusion that the maintenance and extension of the policy of the Commonwealth Arbitration Court in reducing real wages by 10 % is a condition of economic recovery. To this extent policy devised for meeting the crisis should be continued pending the recovery of real income by the long-period expansion of export and protected income.[2]

The currency policy pursued during the depression has also a place in the monetary policy of the immediate future. We have shown in Lectures V and VII how this policy can be sustained without the dangers of inflation. Its objectives are to sustain enterprise, to render elastic the internal financial structure, and to avoid the serious disturbances of unnecessary monetary changes. That it provides a basis for restoring healthy conditions in export production cannot be disputed. By encouraging export production it helps to sustain sheltered production and thus increases the demand for protected production. Moreover, it lowers real costs in industry as a whole and thus assists in the required expansion of protected production competing with imports. The policy should, of course, be left to the Commonwealth Bank to administer with a general direc-

---

[1] Money value may be higher or lower than the pre-depression figure. This is a matter of currency policy, but the real value cannot be restored immediately unless there is a much greater expansion of export and protected income than the most favourable view of present conditions suggests.

[2] The existence of unemployment before the depression reinforces this conclusion and casts doubt upon the ability of the country to avoid further emigration if a fairly large volume of unemployment is not to persist.

tion that currency policy is to aim at promoting a balanced price structure, with as far as practicable general stability after a certain position, say, the 1928 level, has been attained. Early stabilisation of the exchange should be avoided not less than an heroic attempt at restoring parity with sterling. With sterling far removed from its old gold content there can be nothing sacrosanct in parity between the pound Australian and the pound sterling.

Budget policy as laid down in the Premiers' Plan has a long-term application also. Given the general condition of a reduction in real income of the order of 10 % the reductions in expenditure imposed by the Plan must for the present be maintained. We had gone a long way in Australia before the depression in using surplus incomes to support social services. With sur-taxes and relatively high additional taxes for unemployment relief this tendency has been increased.[1] There is little justification for restoration of public expenditure except through a restoration of national income. Certain other budget problems are considered below. Here it is only necessary to indicate that budget economy, like currency and wage policy, though devised to meet the

[1] This point requires closer examination. Reductions in interest and rent, higher taxes on surplus elements in income and special unemployment taxes on income, heavy losses of land rents and declines in the value of equities have all largely taken income from the richer sections of the people. On the other hand, the richer have benefited in some ways from the increase in the value of money and the increase in internal debt. The poorer sections have lost by the fall in real wages and the increase in indirect taxation. The policy of exempting basic needs from the sales tax has, however, kept down the burden of indirect taxation upon the poorer, and the recent decision of the Commonwealth Arbitration Court to adjust wages to movements in the "all items" index number of the cost of living safeguards workers against serious increases in the burden of tariff costs upon their incomes. Reductions in pensions and social services have not on the whole been greater per unit than the fall in the cost of living, while the numbers receiving benefits have increased. Unemployment expenditure has favoured the poor and the fall in the cost of living has provided them compensation for the larger part of their money loss of income. On this rough judgment the crisis policy seems to have increased the proportion of income going to the poorer sections. It would be of great interest to have a careful estimate. In Great Britain the transfer has on the whole been in favour of the richer. See *The Economist*, September 9th, 1933, in commenting on Sykes, *British Public Expenditure*, 1921–31 (King).

special needs of the crisis, must be maintained pending the recovery in export and protected income.

So far the crisis policy has been found to be consistent with the needs of the post-crisis situation. The tariff problem is of a different nature. We have seen above that excessive protection has hampered recovery because it has imposed additional burdens on export production. It can be argued with force that a reduction in duties during the depression would not have injured protected producers. Costs of production have fallen substantially and much more than costs generally abroad. If a given level of duty afforded sufficient shelter before the depression it would be more than adequate, even at parity of exchange, now. But with a depreciated currency the case for lower duties all round is very strong. With higher duties imposed during the crisis in addition to the decline in relative costs and the depreciation of the currency, the revision of the tariff is a first condition of a balanced price structure. In many spheres Australian policy in the crisis has been based upon a certain reduction on the 1928 or pre-crisis standard. This was fundamental in adjustments in wages, interest, government expenditure and rents. It has not been applied to protected income in so far as this income is sheltered by the tariff. On the contrary lower costs and higher duties have favoured this income. It would be folly, as was argued by the 1929 Tariff Committee, to take away duties indiscriminately, and thus to wipe out some protected industries. But there is no danger of injury to protected industry by an all-round reduction in the tariff from the high levels established in 1930. After a general adjustment the task of discriminating among industries to be protected or duties to be reduced should again be committed to the Tariff Board. Substantial changes have already been suggested by the Board, and many of these were incorporated in recent amendments to the tariff. The Board has greatly improved its technique and is now applying the following tests in estimating the degree to which protection should be extended to an industry:

(i) The cost of production of the local industry compared with the cost of imports duty free.

(ii) The capacity of the industry, if given protection from overseas competition, to develop mass production and reduce its costs of production.

(iii) The quality of its product in comparison with the imported product.

(iv) The efficiency of the organisation of the industry and its readiness to pass on the benefits of lower costs to consumers.

(v) The capacity of the industry to employ population and to use Australian raw materials.

(vi) The willingness of the industry to give a guarantee that increased protection will not result in higher prices to the consumer, but that prices will fall if the economies resulting from increased output bring about reduced prices.

But the task of eliminating the more costly industries is also urgent. Where a protected industry imposes heavy costs its abandonment may result in an expansion of other industries more than sufficient to compensate for the loss of employment. An industry may be a net economic burden to a country. Australia cannot at present afford any such industries and complete economic recovery may be long delayed by tariff excesses that maintain costly industries.

VI. *Borrowing and the Burden of Fixed Charges*

Before the depression Australia was spending public loan funds on works at a rate of over £40 m. per annum, or approximately £32 m. at present prices. Her expenditure was reduced to £10 m.—£12 m. in the depression but is to be £17 m. in the current year. This is not excessive and should be within the capacity of the local money market. Two main problems arise in connection with this expenditure. To one considerable publicity has been given for years past; but the other seems to have escaped the attention it deserves. Loan expenditure must be sanctioned by the Loan Council, and the Commonwealth has now accepted ultimate responsibility for the public debt of the States. But the Loan Council is not well equipped to estimate the real economic worth of loan expenditure. In times of acute depression the normal financial standards may be relaxed in the interests of maintaining employment. Australia has, however, had sufficient experience of costly errors in loan expenditure to recognise the need for applying very strict tests to developmental projects financed by public loans. The Loan Council should have independent means of investigating the economic results of proposed expenditure. Before funds are allotted among the governments the projects for expenditure should pass the test of economic soundness much on the lines of modern joint-stock enterprise. Mistakes will still be made (they are common enough in joint-stock enterprise), but they will be fewer and less costly if the prospective results are carefully investigated.

The second problem raises much wider issues, though it is closely related to the first. A large public debt for state enterprises and developmental purposes constitutes a heavy fixed charge that must be met in good and bad times alike. No method has yet been devised whereby the principle of the equity share can be applied to public enterprises. The need for this will become more and more obvious in all parts of the world as the public corporation financed by public bond issues develops. For Australia the problem is already acute. In the depression it was necessary to convert the whole internal public debt to lower rates of interest. A much needed relief on the external debt was obtained through the war debt concession and the conversion of over £100 m. of external debt that fortunately was "callable" or maturing at the time. The most careful in-

vestigation of loan expenditure as suggested above could
not have met this problem, though doubtless it would have
lessened the difficulties caused by the existence of heavy
fixed charges during the depression. The policy of the future
should aim at keeping down the burden of new fixed
charges, especially external, and, if possible, reducing the
old burden. There are several possible lines of action, none
of which is likely to be popular and easy to pursue.

First. Some existing state enterprises might be sold to
private enterprise to lighten the burden of external fixed
charges. The State would be left with some dead weight
debt, but it is carrying this in any case. The principle of the
equity share would be applied by private enterprise and the
dividends to be transferred would rise and fall with the
general prosperity of the country.

Second. A fixed rule could be laid down by the Loan
Council that public borrowing in the future would be confined to the domestic market. Sufficient internal capital
should be available for necessary public works. If sound
enterprises call for new external capital, private enterprise
can be left to explore the field with public assistance by
means of franchises.

Third. In new internal loans or in conversion of external
debt the right of conversion after a certain date at the option of the debtor, with the contingent right of the creditor
to obtain payment at par, might be recognised. This would
be disturbing to the investor, but conversion could not be
successfully attempted unless the debtor's credit were satisfactory. Further, the relief obtainable would be limited to
the prevailing market rate, which would normally be low
in a depression, when the price level had fallen. This
proposal would do rough justice to both parties and render
the burden of fixed interest charges more flexible than at
present.

Fourth. As an alternative to the last proposal the bolder

course of varying the rate of interest up and down according to price changes over stated periods might be adopted. There is the difficulty here of measuring the change in prices, especially in a country with a depreciated currency heavily indebted to one that has retained its old parity with the international standard. But the proposal should prove workable for an internal debt, and would safeguard the investor against currency changes. It would also relieve the debtor in periods of depression and encourage him to be moderate in good times.

Fifth. There is the heroic counsel that debtors with heavy fixed payments should create a substantial reserve in periods of prosperity. Though not a deliberate part of Australian official policy this is precisely what Australia did in the period 1924 to 1929. Her exchange and gold reserves held by the banks were very high at the beginning of the depression and were used for the purpose suggested. Had governments budgeted for surpluses in this period and invested the surpluses in exchange reserves the external effect would have been the same. Internally, however, the budget position would have been much sounder and the difficulties of the crisis lessened.

None of these measures will help to restore national income and employment immediately. All will help to safeguard Australia against the economic and political difficulties associated with the increasing burden of heavy fixed payments in a depression. They will on the whole raise Australian credit abroad, and thus help to secure conversion loans on satisfactory terms in the future. They may be unfamiliar and even in some cases unorthodox, but with the general growth of fixed interest-bearing debt, the international capital markets may have to recognise some method of adjusting fixed interest charges to changing economic conditions.

VII. *Changes in the Australian Economy*

Summarising this discussion as to policy we find that crisis policy should be continued in respect of wage rates, government expenditure and currency control. Tariff policy should be reversed as rapidly as possible to eliminate the more costly of the protected industries and to reduce tariff costs generally. We require a new investment policy on the lines suggested above. Banking policy can develop on lines initiated during the depression with the modifications and extensions suggested in Lecture VII. What fundamental changes in Australian economy will these measures promote and how far will they solve the ultimate problem of recovery? As to changes we may note (*a*) a lowering of the standard of living, (*b*) reduced and more carefully regulated public investment, (*c*) an independent currency policy designed to obtain the maximum advantage from the world recovery in prices, pending the general restoration of an international standard, (*d*) a more flexible structure and money market, (*e*) a substantial reduction in the costs of the tariff, (*f*) a reduction in the burden of fixed interest charges. There is nothing spectacular in these changes, but they should all favour the gradual restoration of private enterprise and investment, and the expansion of export and protected income. In some respects they run counter to the policy now being adopted in the old world and in the United States, but I need not restate the grounds upon which the changes suggested in Australia have been urged. Having gone to excesses in our traditional policy we must now withdraw. The argument that other countries are embracing some of our past heresies has no weight. If they cannot learn by our experience, we at least should have the courage to profit by it.

To what extent are the changes adequate? We have shown that on certain assumptions the restoration of a real national income sufficient to support a standard of living 10% below the pre-crisis level is not impracticable. With strict revision of tariff policy, the relief from tariff costs should cause a net expansion of income and employment in protected and export production and dispel doubts that our fundamental assumptions as to export and protected income are out of keeping with economic possibilities. If, as argued, export and protected income are within £9 m. of the desired goal, unemployment will be much lower than at present, but higher than the pre-crisis level. We cannot foresee all the forces that will operate to influence the amount of the national income. An intensification of economic nationalism in Europe would destroy income in Australia, a relaxation expand it. Increased international trade in the East would provide the needed opportunity for completing the process of recovery with the lower standard of living, and ultimately allow some increase in the standard. This is the most favourable view that can be taken of the future of Australia's economic position.

There are many problems of internal policy and administration that have necessarily been ignored. I must be content with sketching the framework of a national policy. There are, however, other possible courses of action. In particular the effort to increase the degree of socialisation of Australian industry would raise many problems beyond the scope of this discussion. Official policy at the moment is not moving in this direction, and I must plead this as my main reason for ignoring these problems. The extent to which official policy meets the present situation on the lines I have suggested, or on other lines not at present within my ken, will determine the degree to which more radical measures may be attempted.

APPENDIX

STATISTICAL TABLES

I. AUSTRALIAN WHOLESALE AND RETAIL PRICE INDICES

1928 = 100

	Melbourne Wholesale prices	Retail prices: Victoria, food and groceries		Melbourne Wholesale prices	Retail prices: Victoria, food and groceries
1929			**1931**		
Jan.	100·0	102·7	Apr.	80·7	83·7
Feb.	99·2	102·6	May	80·4	82·3
Mar.	100·0	103·8	June	79·5	81·2
Apr.	100·3	104·4	July	79·7	79·8
May	99·6	103·9	Aug.	78·1	79·8
June	100·4	104·7	Sept.	77·6	79·9
July	101·2	104·2	Oct.	78·2	79·3
Aug.	101·9	104·5	Nov.	79·7	80·3
Sept.	103·7	105·4	Dec.	79·5	80·3
Oct.	102·2	107·5			
Nov.	100·7	107·1	**1932**		
Dec.	98·2	101·3	Jan.	78·9	80·9
			Feb.	80·9	82·7
1930			Mar.	80·2	81·5
Jan.	95·9	98·6	Apr.	79·9	81·3
Feb.	93·4	97·8	May	78·6	79·9
Mar.	91·9	97·4	June	77·6	79·0
Apr.	92·7	98·1	July	78·0	78·8
May	93·9	97·9	Aug.	79·0	78·2
June	92·5	97·2	Sept.	80·4	77·8
July	91·7	96·8	Oct.	78·3	76·8
Aug.	90·4	95·9	Nov.	77·1	74·6
Sept.	85·5	93·5	Dec.	76·3	74·2
Oct.	82·5	90·6			
Nov.	80·2	88·4	**1933**		
Dec.	78·1	87·6	Jan.	75·0	72·9
			Feb.	74·2	71·8
1931			Mar.	74·4	70·4
Jan.	88·1	88·4	Apr.	75·8	71·9
Feb.	80·8	86·6	May	78·4	72·8
Mar.	81·3	85·0	June	80·0	74·8

II. Wholesale Prices

1928 = 100

Australia. Commonwealth Statistician's Melbourne index.
United Kingdom. Board of Trade.
United States. Bureau of Labour and Statistics.

	Australia	United Kingdom	United States
1931			
Jan.	81·1	76·2	81·0
Feb.	80·8	75·7	79·5
Mar.	81·3	75·5	78·5
Apr.	80·7	75·4	77·0
May	80·4	74·4	75·4
June	79·5	73·6	74·4
July	79·7	72·9	74·4
Aug.	78·1	71·0	74·4
Sept.	77·6	70·7	73·4
Oct.	78·2	74·4	72·4
Nov.	79·7	75·8	72·4
Dec.	79·5	75·5	70·9
1932			
Jan.	78·9	73·1	69·4
Feb.	80·9	73·1	68·4
Mar.	80·2	74·6	68·4
Apr.	79·9	73·0	67·8
May	78·6	71·8	66·2
June	77·6	69·8	65·8
July	78·0	69·7	66·2
Aug.	79·0	71·0	66·2
Sept.	80·4	72·7	66·2
Oct.	78·3	72·0	66·2
Nov.	77·1	72·0	65·8
Dec.	76·3	72·0	64·8
1933			
Jan.	75·0	71·4	62·8
Feb.	74·2	70·5	61·8
Mar.	74·4	69·5	62·3
Apr.	75·8	69·3	62·0
May	78·4	70·7	64·8
June	80·0	72·2	67·0

III. AUSTRALIAN SHARE PRICE INDICES

May 1926 = 100

	Preference	Banks	Ordinary
1929			
Jan.	102·2	105·9	107·3
Feb.	103·2	105·8	108·3
Mar.	103·5	106·2	106·4
Apr.	103·2	106·7	105·6
May	103·3	106·5	104·7
June	102·8	106·0	102·6
July	103·2	106·2	103·1
Aug.	103·4	104·6	105·6
Sept.	103·1	104·6	104·2
Oct.	100·7	98·1	97·5
Nov.	100·1	95·6	95·1
Dec.	98·1	88·9	91·8
1930			
Jan.	97·3	85·1	83·2
Feb.	95·2	81·4	82·0
Mar.	93·9	81·5	79·7
Apr.	92·9	80·4	77·2
May	92·2	79·8	74·4
June	92·6	80·9	74·7
July	91·4	78·0	67·8
Aug.	89·3	75·4	62·8
Sept.	86·3	70·2	53·6
Oct.	83·6	68·1	53·0
Nov.	83·6	69·4	54·9
Dec.	83·0	65·7	55·0
1931			
Jan.	80·8	60·2	52·1
Feb.	82·1	58·5	53·5
Mar.	82·3	65·5	56·4
Apr.	83·1	67·2	55·9
May	83·1	64·3	55·3
June	82·3	64·2	53·9
July	82·1	63·8	53·1
Aug.	83·1	58·6	51·6
Sept.	81·9	56·4	50·4
Oct.	82·5	60·0	57·4
Nov.	83·8	66·8	63·1
Dec.	86·4	66·6	64·5

IV. BOND AND SHARE PRICE INDICES

1926 = 100

	Yield on Commonwealth Bonds	Price of Ordinary Shares		Yield on Commonwealth Bonds	Price of Ordinary Shares
1931			**1932**		
Jan.	146·1	50·4	May	96·8	62·3
Feb.	152·6	51·7	June	93·0	63·1
Mar.	148·1	54·5	July	84·1	65·8
Apr.	146·2	53·0	Aug.	81·6	71·1
May	176·3	53·2	Sept.	79·7	75·5
June	—	52·1	Oct.	76·7	79·1
July	118·7	51·3	Nov.	73·2	78·7
Aug.	—	49·9	Dec.	75·3	76·3
Sept.	—	48·9	**1933**		
Oct.	108·4	55·5	Jan.	73·8	78·3
Nov.	98·4	61·1	Feb.	73·4	78·4
Dec.	91·1	62·5	Mar.	73·0	78·0
1932			Apr.	71·9	78·8
Jan.	89·0	63·6	May	71·1	80·2
Feb.	92·1	61·3	June	71·2	83·3
Mar.	93·4	60·4	July	70·7	83·8
Apr.	92·5	60·3	Aug.	71·1	85·3

III. AUSTRALIAN SHARE PRICE INDICES (*contd.*)

	Preference	Banks	Ordinary
1932			
Jan.	88·3	65·0	65·7
Feb.	87·6	62·3	63·3
Mar.	86·3	60·0	62·4
Apr.	86·4	59·3	62·3
May	87·6	58·8	64·3
June	88·3	59·5	65·2
July	90·9	60·9	68·0
Aug.	94·7	62·2	73·4
Sept.	98·3	65·7	78·0
Oct.	99·6	67·5	81·7
Nov.	100·9	65·4	81·3
Dec.	101·7	63·0	78·8
1933			
Jan.	103·1	62·0	80·9
Feb.	104·1	59·0	81·0
Mar.	104·2	60·7	80·6
Apr.	103·1	60·7	81·4
May	105·2	62·0	83·9
June	107·1	65·3	86·0
July	106·9	66·4	86·5

VI. Wages and Unemployment

1928 = 100

	Nominal wages	Real wages	Unemployment
1929			
1st qr.	99·8	95·9	86·1
2nd	100·7	96·8	92·6
3rd	100·7	96·8	112·0
4th	100·6	96·5	121·3
1930			
1st	100·5	100·4	135·2
2nd	99·7	100·8	171·3
3rd	98·8	103·6	189·8
4th	96·1	106·6	216·7
1931			
1st	92·4	104·6	238·9
2nd	89·9	104·8	255·6
3rd	88·4	106·9	262·0
4th	86·3	105·9	259·3
1932			
1st	85·6	104·4	262·0
2nd	85·2	105·0	277·8
3rd	81·9	102·8	274·1
4th	81·4	105·2	260·2
1933			
1st	80·8	106·3	245·4

V. The Basic Wage

Commonwealth award for six capital cities

	Nominal wage*	Real wage†		Nominal wage*	Real wage†
1925			**1929**		
1st qr.	94·2	97·9	1st qr.	98·9	95·6
2nd	96·6	98·7	2nd	102·8	99·3
3rd	97·2	98·8	3rd	102·8	99·2
4th	97·7	98·8	4th	102·8	99·1
1926			**1930**		
1st	99·4	98·8	1st	102·8	103·3
2nd	100·0	96·6	2nd	98·9	100·6
3rd	102·8	101·6	3rd	97·7	103·1
4th	100·6	100·0	4th	94·3	104·9
1927			**1931**		
1st	100·0	100·1	1st	80·8	92·0
2nd	99·4	97·8	2nd	78·8	92·4
3rd	98·3	97·5	3rd	76·7	93·3
4th	100·0	98·4	4th	74·1	91·5
1928			**1932**		
1st	101·1	100·6	1st	73·1	89·6
2nd	100·0	99·2	2nd	73·6	91·3
3rd	100·0	100·7	3rd	72·6	91·6
4th	98·9	99·5	4th	71·6	92·4
			1933		
			1st	70·1	92·7
			2nd	72·0	95·6

* Av. 1928 = £4. 8s. 0d. = 100.   † Av. 1928 = 100.

VII. UNEMPLOYMENT BY INDUSTRIES

	Wood, furniture, etc.	Engineering, metal works, etc.	Food, drink, tobacco	Clothing, hats, boots	Books, printing	Other manufactures	Building	Mining, quarrying, etc.	Land transport (not rail or tram)	Miscellaneous	All Groups
1929											
1st qr.	6·5	11·2	5·4	9·8	2·6	13·8	10·6	13·2	7·6	7·3	9·3
2nd	13·6	9·4	11·4	10·2	3·2	17·9	8·8	12·0	8·4	8·3	10·0
3rd	14·2	13·2	11·6	12·8	3·4	20·7	11·9	11·3	9·3	10·1	12·1
4th	15·5	15·4	12·8	10·0	3·3	22·1	14·3	8·6	9·0	11·6	13·1
1930											
1st	20·6	16·7	9·3	12·5	3·8	25·5	17·5	8·7	9·9	12·9	14·6
2nd	25·2	20·5	14·2	16·7	6·8	31·0	23·3	12·2	14·6	15·1	18·5
3rd	21·3	21·9	15·4	21·0	8·4	32·8	25·9	20·8	16·7	16·9	20·5
4th	29·4	25·2	16·8	22·5	10·1	38·7	27·9	28·8	18·5	17·7	23·4
1931											
1st	31·1	27·7	17·4	25·9	12·6	42·3	30·4	32·4	21·9	19·8	25·8
2nd	33·3	30·2	20·7	26·7	14·4	44·3	32·6	32·7	24·0	19·9	27·6
3rd	34·0	31·2	20·5	27·4	15·0	45·0	33·5	33·7	25·5	20·5	28·3
4th	34·8	31·2	20·8	23·9	15·0	42·5	36·0	33·5	25·2	20·2	28·0
1932											
1st	36·6	31·1	17·1	22·8	15·4	42·5	37·9	33·5	27·3	21·4	28·3
2nd	39·6	33·9	19·4	22·6	16·8	43·0	42·1	34·2	29·6	22·2	30·0
3rd	39·4	32·9	20·7	21·3	16·7	41·3	41·6	35·6	29·9	22·0	29·6
4th	38·4	31·6	18·4	17·8	15·6	39·8	40·2	33·7	28·0	21·1	28·1
1933											
1st	36·2	30·2	16·6	17·1	15·8	37·8	38·7	29·1	27·1	19·9	26·5
2nd	35·3	30·0	16·7	17·4	15·9	35·9	36·6	28·1	25·4	19·2	25·7

VIII. Monthly Imports and Exports of Merchandise

(Valued in stg.)

Month	Imports		Exports		Balance	
	1930/31	1931/32	1930/31	1931/32	1930/31	1931/32
	£1,000	£1,000	£1,000	£1,000	£1,000	£1,000
July	7,347	3,081	5,975	4,337	−1,372	+1,256
Aug.	6,834	3,794	4,491	3,293	−2,343	− 501
Sept.	6,115	3,358	5,551	4,601	− 564	+1,243
Oct.	6,904	3,810	7,948	7,070	+1,044	+3,260
Nov.	6,017	3,562	8,283	7,703	+2,266	+4,141
Dec.	5,137	3,655	8,062	8,370	+2,925	+4,715
Jan.	5,084	3,328	5,643	7,184	+ 559	+3,856
Feb.	3,545	3,414	6,309	7,516	+2,764	+4,102
Mar.	4,152	3,803	7,023	7,480	+2,871	+3,677
Apr.	2,855	4,036	6,337	7,124	+3,482	+3,088
May	3,349	3,965	5,199	5,946	+1,850	+1,981
June	3,222	4,276	5,036	4,149	+1,814	− 127
Year	60,561	44,082	75,857	74,773	+15,296	+30,691

Month	1932/33	1933/34	1932/33	1933/34	1932/33	1933/34
July	4,535	4,319	3,892	5,023	− 643	+ 704
Aug.	5,356	4,858	3,039	4,544	−2,317	− 314
Sept.	5,132	4,888	6,327	8,008	+1,195	+3,120
Oct.	5,305		7,171		+1,866	
Nov.	5,663		8,218		+2,555	
Dec.	4,375		8,221		+3,846	
Jan.	4,605		6,964		+2,359	
Feb.	4,366		8,861		+4,495	
Mar.	4,534		8,499		+3,965	
Apr.	4,167		6,495		+2,328	
May	4,193		5,898		+1,705	
June	4,528		4,312		− 216	
Year	56,759		77,897		+21,138	

206

IX. Exchange—Australia on Gold

(Buying price of $486·7)

Average for	£A.	Average for	£A.
1930		**1932**	
Jan.	102	Jan.	177
Feb.	102	Feb.	176
Mar.	104	Mar.	168
Apr.	106	Apr.	162
May	106	May	165
June	106	June	166
July	106	July	171
Aug.	106	Aug.	175
Sept.	106	Sept.	175
Oct.	108	Oct.	180
Nov.	109	Nov.	186
Dec.	109	Dec.	185
1931		**1933**	
Jan.	120	Jan.	181
Feb.	130	Feb.	178
Mar.	130	Mar.	177
Apr.	130	Apr.	169
May	130	May	181
June	130	June	180
July	130	July	182
Aug.	130	Aug.	185
Sept.	139		
Oct.	163		
Nov.	170		
Dec.	180		

X. Percentage Reductions of Expenditure,
1932/33 on 1929/30

(Published in the Report of Premiers' Conference, June 1933)

	Public service proper	All services (including railways)
	%	%
Commonwealth	21·9	21·5
New South Wales	23·4	23·15
Victoria	17·0	20·5
Queensland	15·2	15·1
South Australia	19·0	20·0
Western Australia	19·2	19·2
Tasmania	20·0	19·0

XI. Comparison of Aggregate Revenue and Expenditure, 1929/30, 1931/32, 1932/33 (Probable), 1933/34 (Tentative). Commonwealth and States

(Published in the Report of Premiers' Conference, June 1933)

Expenditure

	1929/30	1931/32	1932/33	1933/34
	£m.	£m.	£m.	£m.
Interest	57·43	53·06	49·56	49·17
Sinking fund	6·22	5·05	5·34	5·71
Exchange	0·14	8·43	7·59	7·19
Unemployment	1·57	11·46	9·21	7·94
Pensions, etc.*	24·02	24·13	23·26	23·33
Salaries and wages	64·42	50·12	48·42	48·92
Commonwealth grants to States†	11·49	12·09	14·77	12·66
All other expenditure	39·35	30·94	30·45	31·32
	204·64	195·28	188·60	186·24

Revenue

	1929/30	1931/32	1932/33	1933/34
	£m.	£m.	£m.	£m.
Taxation	91·86	86·13	90·55	85·18
Business undertakings	70·39	59·18	59·79	60·38
Other revenue	24·18	23·73	23·08	21·68
Commonwealth grants†	8·51	9·15	9·42	9·42
	194·94	178·19	182·84	176·66
Deficit	9·70	17·09	5·76	9·58
	204·64	195·28	188·60	186·24

* Pensions, etc., include Invalid and Old-age, War, Widows, and Public Service Pensions, Maternity Allowances and Family Endowment.
† The difference between Expenditure and Receipts is due to the fact that a portion of the Commonwealth grants is paid to funds outside the Revenue Accounts of the States, e.g. contributions to Sinking Funds.

ADDENDUM

As the book goes to press, a few points of importance in Australian economic policy in the past two months are worthy of brief mention.

(i) The Commonwealth Budget revealed a surplus of £3·5 m. for 1932/33, in conformity with estimates at the end of the year. This was attained despite remissions of taxation and increases in expenditure of £3·25 m. made after the budget was passed. For 1933/34, remissions in taxation of £7·5 m. and restorations of expenditure of £1·7 m. are announced. The tax concessions cover reductions in company tax, income tax, especially on income from property, taxation of insurance companies, land tax, primage and customs duties. They will reduce costs in industry and encourage investment.

(ii) After enquiry, the Tariff Board found that costs generally in industry had fallen substantially despite the depreciation of the currency. It recommended a reduction in duties of one-fourth of the existing duties up to a maximum of 12½%. This formula was not to apply to goods from countries whose currencies were depreciated more than Australian currency. The Government has now applied the Board's recommendations to all protected goods entitled to admission under the British Preferential Tariff. With the 5% remission in primage, the maximum reduction in duties on British goods is 17½%.

(iii) In the budget statement, the Treasurer made the following interesting reference to the future of Australian currency: "It is clear that it will not suit Australia, as a debtor country, for sterling to be over-valued when the time comes to link up again with gold. Whatever the United Kingdom may decide to do in this respect, it is important that we should retain our own right to fix our monetary unit at the point which is consistent with our own price level at the appropriate time".

(iv) The Loan Council decided on November 6th to raise an internal loan of £10 m. at 3½% with an issue price of 99. Half the proceeds were to be devoted to public works and half to funding purposes. This is consistent with the general policy of cheap money and the use of surplus funds to reduce the floating debt. The loan was over-subscribed in two days, a record for Australian internal loans.

(v) Export prices rose from March to September by 40%. Despite the set-back in world prices in October, the Australian export price level is about 35% above the figure for recent years. In particular, wool prices have maintained their advance, the average price at recent sales being over 14*d.* per lb., compared with 8½*d.* in the past two seasons. This recovery in export prices and the improved budget position justify the conclusion reached in Lecture VIII as to the prospects of increasing employment in Australian industry.

November 17*th*, 1933.

INDEX

For EU product safety concerns, contact us at Calle de José Abascal, 56–1°, 28003 Madrid, Spain or eugpsr@cambridge.org.

www.ingramcontent.com/pod-product-compliance
Ingram Content Group UK Ltd.
Pitfield, Milton Keynes, MK11 3LW, UK
UKHW010335140625
459647UK00010B/621